Best Recipes of Ohio Inns and Restaurants

Edited and Compiled by:
Margaret E. Guthrie

Editorial Assistance:
Annie L.J. Saart

First edition.

Library of Congress Catalog Number: 88-70860

ISBN: 0-942495-03-9

Others in this series:
Best Recipes of Wisconsin Inns and Restaurants
Best Recipes of Minnesota Inns and Restaurants
Best Recipes of Michigan Inns and Restaurants

For additional copies of this book, or others in the series, contact:

Amherst Press
A division of Palmer Publications, Inc.
P.O. Box 296
Amherst, Wisconsin 54406

Table of Contents

Preface

Ohio being the fourth book in the series, there is a team in place to produce these books. It consists of my publisher, Chuck Spanbauer, who with his talented and dedicated staff make each book a reality. There is my editorial assistant Annie Saart whose eagle eye catches any omissions, my attorney Michael Davis and finally my three children who are responsible for the maintenance of my sense of humor.

For each book, however, local assistance is necessary in order to find out which are the truly good restaurants, where they are and who owns them and cooks for them. Without this local help there would be no best recipes of anywhere and in Ohio particular thanks go to Patricia Weitzel of *Cleveland Magazine*, Judy Otto Ramlow of Olmstead Falls, Robert B. Smith of *Ohio Magazine*, Bobbie Bruner who showed me German Village in Columbus, and Laura Pulfer of *Cincinnati Magazine*. Without the help of these local "spies" there could be no book. Thank you all.

Introduction

Ohio is the fourth book in the series we are doing on the best recipes of inns and restaurants of the various states of the Midwest.

It is with particular pleasure that I introduce the work of Ohio's chefs to readers and cooks, since I was born in Columbus. My mother came from Columbus and I visited my grandparents with great pleasure all the time I was growing up. Some of my best Columbus memories have to do with food!

It was interesting to go back and see how much had changed and how different things looked. Certainly, Trinity Church, where my parents and aunts and uncles were married looks much smaller to me today than it did when I was a child. The old Maramor Restaurant with its wonderful chocolates is gone, fortunately replaced by other equally wonderful restaurants whose recipes are in this book.

These books are proving to be a thorough education for me in the contemporary preparation and presentation of food. It is interesting to see how professional chefs use our culinary heritage and how they incorporate the new with the old.

It's also reassuring to see that many of the old standbys have endured and are, if anything, better than ever. The newest trend in cooking is game and you will find it here prepared in exciting and different ways. There is a venison pate I recommend and quails prepared as only La Maisonette can do.

Ohio, like Michigan, produces a lot of apples and so you will find good apple recipes in here. Ohio has the largest population of Amish in the country and you will find their influence in some of the recipes contained in this book.

Perhaps most reassuring of all, I have discovered as I travel around that restaurants are increasingly concerned about the quality of the food they prepare. One of Ohio's restaurants raises their own chickens. Many contract with individual farmers for specific crops and products done in a careful and healthy way. In Illinois an inn contracts with a farmer for pigs raised organically and the inn prepares their own sausage, bacon and hams. More and more restaurants who pride themselves on their food are getting away from food over whose quality they have no control. This is a healthy sign, both for the consumer and the individual farmer.

When it comes to desserts, Ohio's chefs take a back seat to no one. There are plenty of rich, decadent chocolate desserts, plenty of apple variations, lots of heavy cream, eggs, sugar, pastry and various liqueurs. In short, all of the things that go into making dessert the lovely conclusive end to a meal with that slight overtone of the forbidden which makes it worth the calories.

Ohio is a varied state and one interesting to explore. From the shores of Lake Erie to the Ohio River, from the Pennsylvania border to the Indiana border there is to see in Ohio that is beautiful and interesting. And there is plenty of good food to sustain the traveler. Herewith samples of that sustenance. Bon Appetit!

****

Before you begin cooking, there are some things you ought to consider. First, Ohio's chefs ask that you read each recipe you intend to re-create all the way through. Be sure you have the ingredients on hand and do not substitute one ingredient for another. Do not substitute canned spinach for fresh, for instance, as has been known to happen. When the recipe calls for Dijon-style mustard, use it, not yellow salad mustard.

Also, a word about ingredients. As in most cookbooks, flour means all purpose white flour. If another flour is called for it will be specified, as in unbleached or whole wheat. Butter means butter—other kinds such as unsalted or whipped will be specified. The same is true of sugar. Unless otherwise specified it is white, granulated sugar. Most of the recipes using heavy cream specify "heavy cream" and the distinction here is important. Some of the large dairies are "ultrapasteurizing" their whipping cream, thus destroying the flavor in favor of longer shelf life. Therefore, recipes in this book call for heavy cream, which is the same thing. The label may say "heavy (gourmet) cream" and if you don't see it, ask for it.

Finally, use the freshest ingredients possible. When a recipe calls for lemon juice or Parmesan cheese, squeeze the juice and grate the cheese. There is no comparison when it comes to taste and flavor. And now, good cooking and good eating!

Brunch

Brunch

This chapter which we have called brunch includes dishes that are suitable for that fashionable meal, as well as dishes that on an Italian menu would be I Primi. I Primi are the choices for the first course of a more elaborate meal.

There is a bit of everything here, reflecting both Ohio's farm heritage and the popular new cuisines that reflect current food trends. This chapter contains corn fritters and spinach ravioli with a filling of scallops, proscuitto and cheese as well as a great deal in between. There's a lot here with which to dazzle your guests at your next brunch or tailgate party.

Country Bean Casserole

½ pound bacon, cooked crisp
½ sausage, browned, crumbled
¼ cup chopped onions
¼ cup chopped celery
10 ounces wax beans, drained
10 ounces green beans, drained
10 ounces pork and beans
10 ounces kidney beans
10 ounces butter beans
½ cup brown sugar, packed
1 tablespoon mustard
½ can (6 ounce) tomato soup

Cook the bacon, crumble and set aside. Cook sausage, drain, crumble and set aside.

Saute the onion and celery in some of the reserved fat until tender. Add the beans, being sure to drain only the wax and green beans before adding to the onion celery mixture.

Add the other ingredients and the cooked bacon and sausage, stirring to blend well. Cook in a covered pot or casserole for 2 hours on medium high heat. Or cook in the oven at 350 degrees for about an hour. Yield: 8-12 servings.

From: **The Apple Farm Restaurant**
262 Pearl Road
Brunswick

Corn Meal Mush Bake
Mamliga cu Branza

1¼ cups yellow cornmeal
1¾ teaspoons salt
1½ cups cold water
4 cups cold water

¼ pound butter
½ pint sour cream
¾ pound Wisconsin brick/
mozzarella cheese

Put 4 cups of cold water to boil while mixing the cornmeal, the salt and the 1½ cups cold water together. When the mixture is thoroughly blended, add to the boiling water, stirring constantly. When it begins to thicken, cover and cook for approximately 30 minutes on simmer, stirring often.

Preheat oven to 350 degrees. Cube the cheese. Put about a ⅓ of the butter in a casserole, add a ½ of the mush mixture. Take ½ the cubed cheese and add to the mush mixture with another third of the butter. Top with ½ of the sour cream. Repeat using the rest of the mush, then the cheese then the sour cream. Bake for 1 hour. Yield: 6 servings.

From: **Dobie's Corner**
Ghent Square
843 Cleveland-Massillion Road
Ghent

Chicken Phyllo Rolls
with Corn Cream Sauce

4 boneless chicken breasts,
  poached, diced
1 pound Gruyère cheese, grated
1 bunch green onions
1 yellow pepper, julienned
2 sheets phyllo pastry*
clarified butter
salt and pepper

*You will need 2 sheets of pastry for each serving.

Poach the chicken breasts, cool and dice into cubes. Slice the green onions and mix with the peppers and the chicken.

Preheat oven to 400 degrees. Brush the sheets of phyllo dough with clarified butter. Season with the salt and pepper.

Place a small portion of the chicken mixture down the center of each sheet of pastry. Fold over the edges and roll up into a cylinder shape. Each roll up should be 1 inch in diameter. These can be refrigerated on wax paper until close to serving time. Allow generous space between each roll.

Brush with clarified butter and bake in the oven till golden brown. Garnish with fresh chopped cilantro and serve on Corn Cream Sauce.

Corn Cream Sauce:
3 quarts cream
6 cloves garlic, minced
12 shallots, minced
1½ cups corn

Reduce cream with the garlic and shallots by boiling until thickened. Add corn, seasoning to taste with salt and pepper. Put some of the corn cream sauce on each plate and place 2 chicken phyllo rolls on each plate. Garnish with the fresh chopped cilantro. Yield: 8 servings.

From: **The 10th Street
Market & Cafe**
1400 West Tenth Street
Cleveland

Corn Fritters

11 ounces cream style corn
1 tablespoon baking powder
1 ounce sugar
1 egg
1 to 1½ cups flour

Mix all ingredients together in the order given. Drop with a dipper into deep hot fat. Fry until golden.
Serve with maple syrup.

From: **Peerless Mill Inn**
319 South Street
Miamisburg

Fruit Fritters

2 cups flour
½ cup powdered sugar
2 teaspoons baking powder
2 eggs, slightly beaten
½ cup milk
2 mashed bananas or ¾ cup crushed pineapple or 2 medium apples, chopped, skin on

Mix together dry ingredients. Add the eggs and milk. Add the fruit and mix well. Drop off a soup spoon into hot fat (about 375 degrees) and fry about 2 minutes on each side. Roll in powdered sugar. Serve hot with maple syrup. Yield: about 24 fritters.

From: **Betsey Mills Club Dining Room**
300 4th Street
Marietta

Lasagna po Pollo Bianco
White Lasagna with Chicken and Mushrooms

2 pounds lasagna noodles,
  cooked al dente
½ pound butter
½ cup flour
1 gallon whole milk
3 tablespoons chicken bouillon
dash pepper
dash salt
1½ pounds fontina cheese
2 pounds ricotta cheese
4 eggs
1 teaspoon garlic salt
2 pounds cooked chicken, cut up
1 pound spinach, chopped
  and drained
1½ pounds sliced mushrooms

In a small saucepan melt the butter and slowly stir in the flour, making a smooth roux.

In a large saucepan combine the milk, the chicken bouillon and ½ of the roux with the salt and pepper. Bring to a boil. This should thicken to the consistency of heavy cream.

Then melt in a ½ pound of the fontina cheese, add the remaining roux, blend to thicken and set aside.

Mix together the ricotta cheese, eggs and garlic salt in a bowl. Blend thoroughly. Set aside.

Preheat the oven to 350 degrees. Cover the bottom of a 9 x 12 inch pan with enough of the sauce so that the lasagna noodles will not stick. Layer the ingredients in this order: First, lasagna noodles, then all of the chicken, enough of the sauce to cover or about ¼. Sprinkle about ⅓ of the remaining fontina cheese over the sauce.

Next, another layer of lasagna noodles, then all of the spinach followed by all of the mushrooms. Again, enough sauce to cover, followed by the fontina cheese. The third layer consists of the lasagna noodles and the remaining sauce.

Cover and bake in the oven for 30 minutes. Uncover and bake another 15 minutes. Add the rest of the fontina cheese on top to melt. Heat the rest of the sauce to serve over the lasagna at the table. Yield: 8 servings.

From: **The Fig Tree**
909 Vine Street
Cincinnati

Saffron Ravioli

4 cups flour
2 grams saffron
3 ounces hot water
2 or 4 eggs

Filling:
1 pound cooked lobster meat
1 pound cooked crawfish meat
2 ounces chopped chives
1 pound grated Gouda cheese
2 eggs
salt and pepper to taste

Soak the saffron in the hot water for approximately 45 minutes or until the water turns red.

In the food processor or mixer add flour, saffron and water, adding eggs 1 at a time until dough starts to ball up. If dough is too tacky add more flour until it is firm, then follow instructions in Spinach Ravioli recipe for rolling out ravioli pasta and filling.

For the filling combine the lobster, crawfish, chives, grated cheese and eggs, adding salt and pepper to taste. Fill the raviolis and follow instructions for cooking.

From: **The Baricelli Inn**
2203 Cornell Road
Cleveland

Spinach Ravioli
with Scallops, Proscuitto and Cheese

Ravioli:
4 cups flour
6 cups raw spinach
3 egg yolks

Filling:
60 whole scallops
½ pound proscuitto
3 ounces ricotta cheese
3 ounces mascarpone cheese
3 ounces wilted spinach
3 ounces chopped scallops

For the dough, first wash spinach thoroughly, remove stems. Wilt by putting in a heavy saucepan with a lid over high heat and shaking pan back and forth quickly. Place in food processor or blender and puree until fine. Remove and strain, reserving liquid.

Add the spinach and flour 1 cup at a time to the food processor or mixer. Add 3 tablespoons of the reserved liquid with the egg yolks, mix well. If too wet, add more flour.

Roll out 1 rectangular sheet of dough for the ravioli. Partly score the sheet in 2- to 3-inch squares. Put 2 or 3 teaspoons of filling in each square. Roll out second sheet and place over first, pressing down around each lump of filling. Using a pizza wheel or pie crust cutter, cut along the lengthwise edges to seal the dough. Then cut across to seal and separate each ravioli. Place on rack and allow to dry.

For the filling: Steam the scallops for 1 minute, wrap each in proscuitto. Mix ricotta, mascarpone, spinach and chopped scallops together. Place a bit on each ravioli rectangle, top with a scallop and seal.

Have a pot of boiling, salted water ready. Drop the ravioli, a few at a time, into the water, careful not to disturb the boiling. The raviolis will float to the top when they are done.

From: **The Baricelli Inn**
2203 Cornell Road
Cleveland

Sun-Dried Ravioli
with Crabmeat Chèvre Filling

Ravioli:
4 cups flour
4 teaspoons tomato paste
15 (approximately) sun-dried
  tomatoes
2 eggs

Filling:
2 pounds jumbo crabmeat
salt and pepper to taste
1 pound chèvre frais (goat cheese)

Chop the tomatoes in the food processor. Add the tomato paste and 2 egg yolks. Add the flour 1 cup at a time until the dough begins to ball up. Continue adding flour until the dough is firm.

Follow the instructions in the previous recipe for Spinach Ravioli for making the raviolis.

For the filling, pick over the crabmeat carefully, removing any membranes and bits of shell that might be in the meat. Mix the meat with crumbled cheese and season with salt and pepper to taste. Proceed with making the raviolis.

From: **The Baricelli Inn**
2203 Cornell Road
Cleveland

Reuben Quiche

1 10-inch unbaked pie shell
3 tablespoons finely diced onion
6 ounces corned beef
1 cup sauerkraut, drained
6 ounces grated Swiss cheese
5 eggs
2½ cups half & half cream

Preheat oven to 375 degrees. Evenly distribute onion, corned beef and sauerkraut over the bottom of the unbaked pie shell. Sprinkle cheese over the onion, beef and sauerkraut. Whip the eggs, adding sugar and cayenne pepper. Combine with cream, pour slowly over ingredients in the pie shell. Place

1 tablespoon sugar
dash of cayenne pepper

on baking sheet and bake in the oven until lightly browned and a knife inserted halfway between side and center comes out clean. Yield: 6-8 servings.

From: **Hulbert's Restaurant**
1033 Bridge Street
Ashtabula

Spanakopita

3 pounds fresh spinach
1 bunch green onions, chopped
4 tablespoons olive oil
1½ pounds feta cheese
1 cup cottage cheese
8 eggs, slightly beaten
1 pound phyllo dough
½ pound melted butter

Wash, remove stems and chop spinach. Saute onions in sauce pan with olive oil until soft. Add chopped spinach and mix well. Cook until wilted and excess water evaporates. Set aside.

In a large bowl combine feta cheese, cottage cheese and eggs. Add spinach mixture and mix well.

Preheat oven to 350 degrees. In a buttered 12 x 15 inch pan lay pastry sheets, brushing each sheet with melted butter, until ½ the phyllo dough is used. Spread filling mixture evenly on phyllo and continue to cover with pastry sheets and butter.

Score the top layer with a serving design. Bake for 45 minutes to 1 hour.

From: **Linardo's Villa**
2230 East Main Street
Springfield

Tortellini with Cucumber and Crème Fraîche

This dish is very easy to fix. The sun dried tomatoes will give it a special flavor, although using fresh tomatoes in season is possible.

10 ounces frozen or dried
  spinach stuffed tortellini
3 tablespoons unsalted butter
½ cup sliced mushrooms
½ cup cucumber, peeled,
  seeded and sliced
2 sun-dried tomatoes, sliced thin
  OR ½ cup tomato, peeled,
  seeded and diced
1 cup crème fraîche
½ cup grated Swiss and
  Parmesan cheese, mixed
2 egg yolks

Cook the pasta in boiling, salted water until al dente or about 20 minutes. Drain and toss with 3 tablespoons of olive or vegetable oil. Set aside.

Heat a medium skillet, add the butter, saute mushrooms, cucumbers and tomatoes until translucent, about 5-6 minutes.

Add the pasta and crème fraîche. Stir well. Cook for 3 minutes, add the egg yolks and cheeses. Bring to a boil. Stir well to blend the cheeses and cream together.

Sprinkle with chopped fresh parsley or basil. Serve hot.

From: **Lock 24 Restaurant**
State Route 154
Elkton

Bread & Rolls

Bread and Rolls

There is not a meal ever served that wasn't improved by the addition of a good bread. The best bread can serve as a meal in itself. Certainly when well done bread adds interest to the meal and may also serve to soak up gravies and sauces so the flavors are not wasted.

So there's a lot to be said for bread, but perhaps best to let it speak for itself. Here, then, are some of the best served in Ohio's restaurants.

Brioche Dough

2 cups milk
¾ pound butter
¼ cup sugar
2 tablespoons dry yeast
4 teaspoons salt
3 eggs, room temperature
8 cups flour
3 tablespoons vegetable oil

In a heavy saucepan, bring milk, butter, sugar to a boil. Remove from heat and cool to lukewarm. Put mixture in a large mixing bowl and mix in the yeast completely. Let stand 10 minutes. Yeast will "proof," that is bubble up, indicating that it's active. Beat the eggs, which are at room temperature and add to the mixture in the bowl along with the salt. Blend well. Add the flour, one cup at a time until you have added seven cups. Mix until the dough pulls away from the side of the bowl.

Sprinkle the last cup of flour on a table or pastry board. Put the dough on the flour and knead in the last cup of flour, until the dough is thoroughly mixed. The dough should be elastic and smooth.

Place the dough in a bowl oiled with the vegetable oil, turn to coat completely. Place the bowl in the warmest area of the kitchen. Cover with a clean cloth as this prevents a skin from forming. Let rise until triple in size. Punch down and knead for two minutes. Return to bowl and let rise again until double in size.

Punch down dough and prepare to roll out individual brioche or one large one. To roll one large brioche, take ¾ of the dough and roll with floured hands to form one large roll. Take the remaining ¼ of the dough, shape into a roll also, then make it pear-shaped. With your finger or a chopstick, poke a hole down in the center of the larger roll and insert the slender end of the pear-shaped piece of dough into the hole, until it is joined.

To make smaller brioche, simply do the same thing, rolling each one with the palm of one hand and placing in small fluted brioche molds. Top the same way. Cover with a clean cloth and set in a warm place to rise.

Preheat oven to 425 degrees. When the dough has risen by $\frac{1}{3}$, brush the tops with beaten egg, being careful not to flatten the little tops. Place in oven and cook for 20-25 minutes, watching to see that they don't brown too quickly. To test for doneness, insert the thin blade of a knife under the top. If it comes out clean, the rolls are done. Do not unmold until cool as brioche will lose its shape.

This brioche recipe is used at Ziggy's for all their en croute recipes like coulibiac.

From: **Ziggy's**
Continental Restaurant
3140 Riverside Drive
Columbus

Sunday Cinnamon Rolls

Cinnamon rolls are one of the current "in" foods. Most of us never knew they were out. Here's the real thing—a fond memory from childhood for most of us!

1 package dry yeast
¼ cup warm water
   (110-115 degrees)
1 cup milk, scalded
2 tablespoons sugar
2 tablespoons butter
1 teaspoon salt
3½ cups sifted flour
1 egg

Filling:
½ cup brown sugar
¼ cup melted butter
1½ teaspoons cinnamon

Sticky Topping:
½ cup light or dark corn syrup
¼ cup brown sugar
¼ cup melted butter
½ teaspoon cinnamon

Soften the yeast in the warm water. Combine the scalded milk, sugar, butter and salt; mix well and cool to lukewarm. Add 1 cup of the flour; beat well. Beat in softened yeast and the egg. Gradually add the remaining flour to form a soft dough.

Place in a greased bowl, turning to coat the dough. Cover with a clean towel and let rise in a warm place till double in bulk. Preheat oven to 350 degrees. Punch down and turn out onto a lightly floured surface. Divide the dough in half. Roll out each half in a rectangular shape approximately 16 x 8 inches. Spread the surface with filling. Roll lengthwise. Seal edge, cut in 1-inch slices. Mix together the topping ingredients and place in well greased pan. Place roll slices cut side down in pan on the topping. Let rise until double in bulk.

Bake in oven for 20-25 minutes or until golden brown. While still warm, turn pan upside down on baking tray so topping may run down sides of rolls. Serve warm. May be cooled to be frozen. Reheat in oven or microwave.

From: **Hulbert's Restaurant**
1033 Bridge Street
Ashtabula

Arnold's Special Pita Toasts

pita bread, cut in triangles
garlic butter*
freshly grated Romano cheese

*Garlic butter:
$1/3$ cup butter
3 garlic cloves, chopped
$1/3$ cup olive oil
$1/3$ salad oil

For the toasts, cut plain pita bread in triangles, then split the triangles so each triangle is a single layer. Place on a cookie sheet with the inside of the bread facing up.

Brush each piece with the garlic butter. Sprinkle with the freshly grated Romano cheese and bake at 400 degrees for 10 minutes or just until golden brown.

For the garlic butter, melt the butter in a heavy saucepan. Add the chopped garlic and let slowly simmer for about 5 minutes. The garlic should not brown, but needs the time to release all its flavor. Turn off the heat and add both the oils. This will keep in the refrigerator for 2 weeks or more. It also makes a superb saute base.

From: **Arnold's Bar & Grill**
210 East Eighth Street
Cincinnati

Red Pepper Rolls

2 red peppers, roasted
2 tablespoons tomato puree
1 tablespoon sugar
1 teaspoon paprika
$3/4$ cup warm water
   (110-115 degrees)
$1 1/2$ packages dry yeast*
4 cups flour
$1/2$ cup corn meal, semolina
2 teaspoons salt

Roast the peppers, skin, seed and puree. Place ingredients in a large mixing bowl in the above order. Mix till dough forms a ball and pulls away from the sides of the bowl. Continue mixing for about 4 minutes.

Place dough in greased bowl, turn to coat evenly, cover with clean towel and let rise in a warm place for approximately 1 hour.

Shape the rolls and let rise again for about 45 minutes. Preheat oven to 375 degrees.

½ cup chopped green onions
2 tablespoons olive oil

*one package yeast is equivalent to 1 tablespoon.

Place rolls in oven and bake for about 20 minutes.

From: **The 10th Street Market & Cafe**
1400 West 10th Street
Cleveland

Rosemary Bread

4 ounces warm water
   not to exceed 114 degrees
¼ ounce yeast
1 teaspoon sugar
2 ounces onion, pureed
1 teaspoon rosemary
½ ounce bacon grease
2 ounces cold milk
1 teaspoon salt
10 ounces flour

In a mixing bowl with the warm water, add the yeast, sugar, onion, rosemary and bacon fat. Let stand for 4 minutes for the yeast to activate.

Add the cold milk, salt and mix together with a dough hook.

Add the flour and knead for 12 minutes.

Let dough rest for 15 minutes. Divide and shape the dough into 2 8-ounce loaves, put on greased cookie sheet. Let rise for approximately 45 minutes.

Preheat oven to 350 degrees. Brush loaves with an egg wash made with an egg beaten with a little water. Bake in the oven for approximately 20 minutes or until golden brown. Bread should sound hollow when rapped with a knuckle. Serve warm. Yield: 2 loaves.

From: **The Chadwick Inn**
301 River Road
Maumee

Sourdough Bread

Starter:
¾ pound flour
1½ tablespoons sugar
½ ounce dry yeast
2¾ cups water

Bread:
2¾ cups water, 40 degrees
1½ cups starter
½ ounce salt
2¾ pounds flour

For the starter, mix all the ingredients together and let stand at room temperature for 7-8 days. Leave uncovered the first 3 days, then cover for the last 4-5. Temperature should be 72-80 degrees.

For the bread, mix the water and starter by hand in a large mixing bowl. Add the salt, then the flour, mixing at medium speed. Let the dough reach room temperature and double in size.

Refrigerate overnight. Let the dough reach room temperature, then shape into loaves, cover and let rise in a warm place. Preheat oven to 400 degrees. Bake 35-45 minutes. Yield: 2 two pound loaves.

From: **Rigsby's
Cuisine Volatile**
692 North High Street
Columbus

Appetizers

Appetizers

Appetizers are just what their name implies; something to whet the appetite, something to introduce the meal to follow, letting you know you're in for a treat.

Ohio's chefs have done themselves proud here, with both dishes to tease the palate and satisfy the appetite. Some of these appetizers could well make a meal by themselves. Well, with the addition of a judiciously chosen bottle of wine, suitably crunchy bread and a good, green salad, they certainly could.

And these recipes are marvelous additions for your entertaining file. Try some and see if you don't agree.

Hot Spiced Cider

Ohio is big in the production of apples. Here's a mulled cider recipe from the heart of apple country.

1 gallon cider
2 large cinnamon sticks
½ teaspoon whole allspice
½ teaspoon whole cloves
¾-1 cup fresh lemon juice

Put all ingredients in a large stainless steel or enamel stockpot and bring to a boil. Remove from heat and serve.

From: **The Welshfield Inn**
Route 422
Welshfield

Country Pate

1 pound boneless pork shoulder
1 pound boneless veal shoulder
½ pound fresh pork fat
4 shallots, chopped
2 large garlic cloves, minced
3 bay leaves
¼ teaspoon allspice
salt to taste
freshly ground black pepper
   to taste
1 rounded teaspoon thyme
¼ cup brandy
¾ cup white wine
3 large eggs
¾ pound good bacon

Coarsely grind the pork, veal and pork fat together. Add the chopped shallots, the garlic, then the bay leaves, allspice, salt and pepper, and thyme. Add the brandy and the wine. Mix well, cover and refrigerate for 2 days, stirring once a day.

Preheat oven to 300 degrees. Adjust the seasoning and mix in eggs. Line a 2-quart terrine with the bacon and spoon the pate mixture into the terrine, pack tightly and cover with the remaining bacon. Bake in the preheated oven for 2 hours. Let the pate cool in the refrigerator overnight. Put a 4-pound weight on top.

Slice and place on serving platter, garnish with fresh watercress and cornichons. Yield: 10-12 servings.

From: **L'Auberge**
4120 Far Hills Avenue
Dayton

Three Cheese and Herb Strudel

½ pound feta cheese
¼ pound cream cheese
¼ pound cottage cheese
⅛ teaspoon garlic powder
⅛ teaspoon freshly grated
   black pepper
½ teaspoon dill seed
1 tablespoon chopped parsley
1 tablespoon chopped scallions
10 sheets of phyllo dough

clarified butter
sesame seeds

Combine the first eight ingredients until well mixed. Brush each sheet of phyllo dough with clarified butter.

Preheat oven to 400 degrees. Place 2 sheets together to make 5 double layers of dough. With knife, cut sheets in half lengthwise. Divide the cheese mixture into 10 portions. Place portion of cheese mixture onto center of phyllo dough. Turn up edges of the dough to secure the sides. Roll as you would for an egg roll. Brush strudels with butter and sprinkle with sesame seeds on top. Bake on buttered sheet pan for 12-15 minutes or until dough is crisp. Yield: 10 appetizers or 5 entree servings.

From: **Grammer's Restaurant**
1440 Walnut Street
Cincinnati

Eggplant Terrine

4 medium to large eggplant,
  peeled and sliced
1 teaspoon marjoram
1 teaspoon basil
1 teaspoon thyme
1 teaspoon oregano
12 red peppers
12 yellow peppers

Slice the eggplants approximately ⅛-inch thick. Salt sliced eggplant with kosher salt and weigh down to press out all moisture. Leave for ½ hour. Rinse, then pat dry.

Fry the eggplant in olive oil until golden brown. Drain on paper towels. Grill peppers by impaling on the tines of a cooking fork over a gas flame and then peel off skin. Remove seeds and membranes, slice.

Preheat oven to 350 degrees. Line a terrine with parchment paper. Put down a layer of eggplant, sprinkle with the herbs, then follow with a layer of multi-colored peppers. Follow the same procedure until all the eggplant and peppers are gone.

Put the terrine in a bain marie for 45 minutes. Let cool while weighed down with another terrine filled with beans or other heavy material. A bain marie is a hot water bath using a slightly larger pan and making sure the hot water is at least halfway up the sides of the terrine.

When cool, slice and serve. Garnish with fresh red and yellow peppers, watercress or any fresh greens.

From: **The 10th Street
Cafe & Market**
1400 West 10th Street
Cleveland

Moules a la Crème Safranée
Mussels with Cream and Saffron

3 pounds of mussels,
  washed and bearded
½ cup white wine
¼ cup chopped shallots
½ quart heavy cream
6 strands saffron
salt and pepper to taste

Place the cleaned mussels and wine in a large non-reactive saucepan. Allow enough room to let the mussels open. Steam mussels in the wine for 4-5 minutes or until all shells open.

Remove mussels and reserve liquid. Remove the mussels from their shells and discard the shells. Strain the reserved liquid through cheesecloth to remove any sand. In a non-reactive, heavy bottomed saucepan put shallots in liquid, reduce liquid by half. Add the heavy cream and saffron and reduce by half again.

Place the shucked mussels and the chopped parsley in the reduced cream mixture, salt and pepper to taste. Serve. Yield: 6 servings.

From: **L'Armagnac
Restaurant Francais**
121 South Sixth Street
Columbus

Romanian Ground Fingerlings
Mititei

1 pound ground veal
1 pound ground round steak
1 pound ground lamb
1½ cups chicken broth or
   beef broth
½ cup dried parsley flakes
1 tablespoon garlic powder
1 teaspoon freshly ground
   black pepper

Mix all the ingredients together and add additional hot water, if necessary, so that the mixture is moist but not runny or soupy. Form into fingerlings. Make them larger for rare, smaller and thinner for well done. Grill or broil to taste.

From: **Dobie's Corner**
           Ghent Square
           843 North Cleveland-
           Massillion Road
           Ghent

Sauerkraut Balls

1 pound mashed potatoes*
1½ pounds sauerkraut,
   wrung out
4 ounces finely chopped ham
1 tablespoon chopped parsley
2 tablespoons chopped scallions
1 tablespoon mustard
salt and pepper to taste
flour, egg wash, and
   fresh bread crumbs

*Note: cook potatoes, mix with 1
teaspoon butter and a little milk,
salt and pepper.

Combine all the ingredients except the flour, egg wash and fresh bread crumbs. Mix well and shape into 1-inch diameter balls. Bread with flour, then the egg wash, made with an egg beaten with a little water or milk, then roll in the fresh bread crumbs. Deep fry or pan fry until golden brown.

From: **Grammer's Restaurant**
1440 Walnut Street
Cincinnati

Venison Paté
with Cumberland Sauce

4 ounces veal
5 ounces pork
6 ounces venison
5 ounces button mushrooms
3½ ounces apples
2 ounces onions
6 ounces chicken livers
8 ounces bacon
5½ ounces fat back

Grind the veal, pork and venison. Wash the fresh mushrooms and let drain. Peel and rough chop the apples and onions. On a grill or in a large skillet, saute the chicken livers, bacon, fat back, mushrooms, apples and onions lightly—about 5 minutes over medium heat. Grind the sauteed ingredients. Mince the garlic and crush the juniper berries and add to the mixture. Add the other

1 teaspoon minced garlic
5 juniper berries
pinch fresh black pepper
1 teaspoon salt
1 tablespoon Madeira
1 tablespoon brandy
¼ cup egg whites
12 slices good bacon
baker's twine

seasonings, mix in the ground meats, then add the Madeira, brandy and egg whites and blend well.

Preheat oven to 300 degrees. Lightly pound the 12 slices of bacon and line the inside of a terrine, reserving two slices. Add enough forcemeat (the mixture you've just made) to fill half the mold. On a hard, level surface raise the mold about 6 inches and let it fall flat. This settles the mixture. Repeat this three times. Fill the rest of the mold, raise and let fall three more times to settle the top half. Fold over any excess bacon hanging out the edges on top of the forcemeat. Use the two reserved slices of bacon to cover the top of the forcemeat. Cover the bacon with plastic wrap, put the lid on the terrine and tie down with baker's twine. Place the terrine in a water bath (bain marie) and bake in the oven until the internal temperature reaches 130 degrees. Yield: 1 terrine or 20 slices.

Cumberland Sauce:
½ cup fresh lemon juice
½ cup fresh orange juice
julienne peels of 2 oranges and
    2 lemons
1 pound red currant jelly
1¼ cups port wine
1 tablespoon English mustard
pinch cayenne pepper
pinch ginger

Mix the two juices and the julienne peels together in a non-reactive saucepan and cook over low heat, reducing by half. Once reduced, remove from heat and let stand for 2 minutes. With a whip blend the rest of the ingredients into the juice peel mixture. Yield: 1 quart of sauce, enough for 1 terrine.

To serve the pate with the sauce, pour a little sauce on each service plate and place a slice of venison pate on the sauce. Garnish with watercress, or any fresh, crisp green.

From: **Ziggy's**
Continental Restaurant
3140 Riverside Drive
Columbus

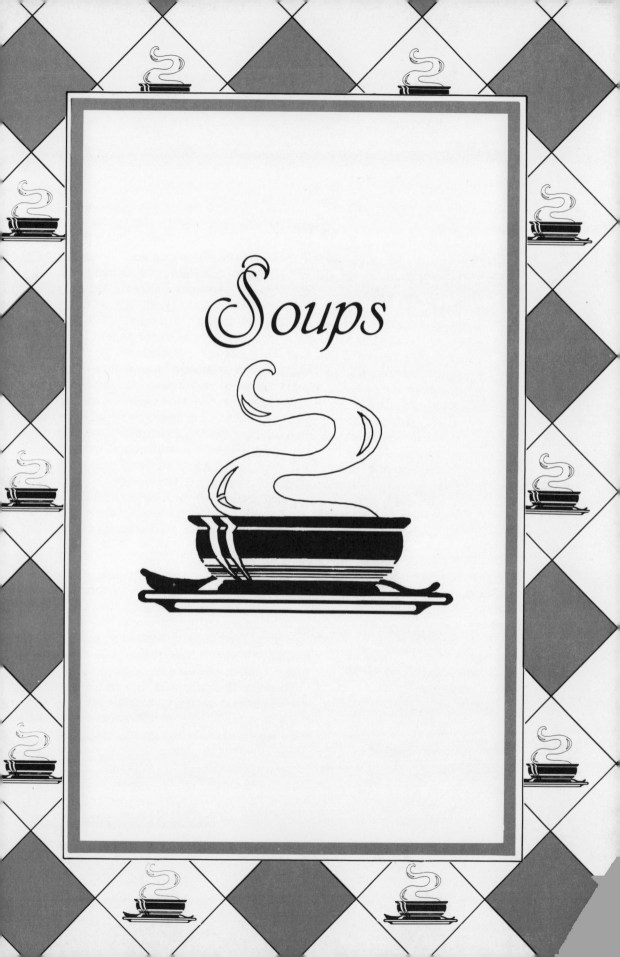

Soups

Soups

Soups would seem to be a specialty of almost every cuisine and ours is no exception. Ohio's chefs have submitted some of their best recipes for you to try.

One of the most appealing attributes of making soup is that it is a forgiving dish. It is easy to correct mistakes most of the time—for instance, if you've put too much salt, just add a couple of peeled whole potatoes to the soup and let simmer for a few minutes. Then remove the potatoes. Also, with soups that call for many ingredients, if one or two are missing or must be substituted for, there is usually not much difference in the end product. Soup is a good teacher, too, a good way of learning what flavors and textures will go together.

All you need to enjoy Ohio soups is a hearty appetite!

Beef Stock

3 pounds beef, veal bones
1 large onion, quartered, skin on
2 carrots, cut in large chunks
2 celery stalks, with leaves
2 tablespoons fresh thyme
1 bay leaf
2 tablespoons tomato paste
4 sprigs parsley, stems only
6 cups water

*Note: This stock can be frozen and kept in the freezer up to 3 months.

Place bones, onion, carrots, celery, bay leaf and thyme in a large shallow roasting pan. Bake in a 450-degree oven for about 45 minutes or until the bones are well browned, turning occasionally.

In a large stock pot place all browned ingredients. Add parsley, tomato paste and water. Bring to a boil. Reduce heat and let stock simmer for 3 to 4 hours, skimming frequently, adding more water as needed.

Remove from heat, lift out bones and vegetables with a slotted spoon. Strain the stock through a sieve. Skim off fat with a spoon or chill the stock and lift off the solidified fat. Makes about 5 cups.

From: **Lock 24 Restaurant**
State Route 154
Elkton

Black Bean Soup

4 cups dried black beans
8 cups water
3 cloves chopped garlic
1 medium onion, chopped
3 ribs celery, chopped
1 green pepper, chopped
¼ cup salad oil
1 teaspoon crushed red pepper
½ cup dry sherry
1 tablespoon dry mustard
salt to taste
¼ cup lemon juice

2 finely chopped hard boiled eggs

Carefully pick through the beans for small stones, then rinse the beans and place in soup pot with about 8 cups of water. Bring to a boil, then turn off heat and cover the pot with a lid for 1 hour.

While beans are sitting, saute the garlic, onions, celery, and bell pepper in salad oil until just soft, then add to the black beans. Bring to a slow simmer over low heat and simmer until the beans are just soft. If soup becomes too thick, add more water.

When beans are soft add sherry, dry mustard, lemon juice and salt.

Take a good look at the soup. If too thick, thin with water. If too thin thicken by putting part of soup through the blender and adding back.

Serve topped with chopped, hard-boiled egg.

From: **Arnold's Bar & Grill**
210 East Eighth Street
Cincinnati

Cauliflower and Cheddar Chowder

1 cup butter
1 cup chopped celery
1 cup chopped onions
¾ cup flour
1 quart milk
1 quart half & half
½ head cauliflower
2 cups chicken stock
2 cups diced, cooked potatoes
8 ounces grated sharp
  Cheddar cheese
salt and pepper to taste

Melt butter in heavy 6-quart stock pot. Saute celery and onions until tender. Remove from heat and stir in flour. Cook 1 to 2 minutes. Stir in milk and half & half. Cook until thick. Steam cauliflower, broken into florettes, in the chicken stock. Reserve 1 cup liquid and add to the chowder base. Add cauliflower, potatoes and seasonings to chowder base. Simmer for 10 minutes. Stir in grated cheese. Garnish with fresh parsley. Yield: 12 servings.

From: **Peerless Mill Inn**
319 South Second Street
Miamisburg

Cream of Eggplant Soup

3 tablespoons olive oil
6 cloves garlic
6 shallots, chopped
2 medium onions, diced
2 ribs celery
1 carrot
2 medium eggplant,
    peeled and diced
1 tomato, skinned and diced
salt and pepper to taste
1 teaspoon dried thyme or
    2 teaspoons fresh
1 cup sherry
1½ cups chicken stock
½ cup heavy cream
3 tablespoons parsley,
    chopped for garnish

In a large stockpot, put olive oil. Over medium heat roast the garlic cloves until light brown, then add the shallots and onions and cook for 5 minutes, stirring occasionally.

Add the celery, carrot, eggplant, tomato, herbs, salt and pepper and cook for another 5 minutes, stirring occasionally. Now add the sherry and chicken stock and bring to a boil. Reduce the heat and simmer for 35 minutes. Let the soup cool and then puree in the blender or food processor. Strain through a medium strainer.

Bring to a boil, add the cream. Adjust the seasoning with salt and pepper. Serve garnished with the chopped parsley. Yield: 6 8-ounce servings.

From: **L'Armagnac
Restaurant Francais**
121 South Sixth Street
Columbus

Light Cream of
Green Lentil Soup
with Celery

1½ cups green lentils
3 tablespoons unsalted butter

Wash and soak lentils overnight. Drain, set aside. Melt the butter in a large stockpot and

1 medium celery root, peeled and
   cut into 1-inch julienne
1 medium leek, white part only,
   cleaned and cut ⅛-inch slices
2 shallots, coarsely chopped
1 clove garlic, mashed
3 tablespoons olive oil
½ small bunch watercress,
   stems removed
juice of 1 lemon
2 teaspoons Dijon-style mustard
1 tablespoon red wine vinegar
½ cup heavy cream

2 slices white bread,
   cut into ½-inch cubes

add the celery root peelings, leek, shallots and garlic. Cook over medium heat until just wilted, about 5 minutes.

Add lentils to the cooked vegetables and mix well. Pour in 1½ quarts water, season with salt and pepper. Bring to a boil. Reduce the heat to low, and simmer for 1 hour. Add watercress leaves to soup during the last 5 minutes of cooking.

In the meantime, place celery root julienne in a non-reactive saucepan filled with cold water. Add the lemon juice and bring to a boil. Cook until tender, about 10 minutes. Drain in a non-reactive sieve or colander and set aside.

In a medium skillet, heat olive oil until hot. Add the bread cubes and fry over high heat until uniformly brown, about 2 minutes. Drain on paper towels.

Working in batches, if necessary, pour soup into a food processor or blender and puree until creamy. Pass through a fine mesh sieve into a medium saucepan and bring to a simmer over low heat. Add the mustard and vinegar. Pour in cream and season with salt and pepper. Add julienne of celery root. Serve with croutons and additional cream, if desired. Yield: 8 servings.

From: **Ziggy's**
Continental Restaurant
3140 Riverside Drive
Columbus

Rigsby's
Onion and Garlic Soup
with Toasted Brie Crouton

This soup is a favorite of local food writers, cooking teachers and restaurant critics!

4½ pounds veal leg bones*,
  cut into 2-inch pieces
2 large white onions, diced
  but not peeled
2 large carrots, diced
  but not peeled
2 ribs of celery, diced
¼ cup tomato paste
4 medium white onions,
peeled and diced
1 ounce clarified butter
1 teaspoon minced garlic
2 ounces sherry
salt and pepper to taste
3-4 ounces Brie, cut into 4-6 slices
4-6 slices sourdough bread

*Note—veal bones may be some-
what difficult to locate, but should
be available at butcher shops
upon request.

To prepare the stock, roast the veal leg bones at 475 degrees for 2½ hours or until well browned. During the last hour add the first amount of onions, the carrots and celery to the roasting pan with the bones.

Remove the roasted bones and vegetables from the pan and deglaze pan with enough water to liquify drippings from pan. Place roasted bones, vegetables, and deglazing liquid into a pot that is large enough so that the bones and vegetables will come up only halfway to the rim. Add tomato paste and 4½ quarts of water, or enough to cover the bones and vegetables by 4-5 inches.

Bring the stock to a boil; then reduce to a simmer. Continue to simmer for 8-10 hours, skimming frequently. Replenish with water as needed.

Strain stock through a fine sieve into a clean pot. Simmer until stock is reduced by half or until it yields 1½ quarts. Continue to skim broth throughout the entire process. At this point stock may be used to complete the soup. It may also be refrigerated for 4-5 days or frozen for 2-3 weeks.

To complete the soup, in large pot saute the second amount of onions in butter until translucent, add the garlic and continue to

cook for 2 minutes. Add the stock and bring to a boil. Reduce to a simmer and remove any sediment. Reduce soup until it is slightly thickened. Season with sherry, salt and pepper.

To prepare the sourdough croutons, divide the slices of brie evenly over bread slices and broil briefly until cheese melts. Ladle soup into individual bowls. Place 1 sourdough crouton on top of each bowl. Yield: 4-6 servings.

From: **Rigsby's
Cuisine Volatile**
692 North High Street
Columbus

Philadelphia Pepper Pot Soup

This soup is supposed to have originated with George Washington during the long winter at Valley Forge. Washington is said to have asked his cook to create a satisfying dish that would sustain his men and renew their morale. Using what ingredients came to hand, the cook came up with Pepper Pot Soup. Washington added the Philadelphia in honor of the cook's birthplace.

2 ounces diced bacon
2 green onions, chopped
½ green pepper, chopped
1 tablespoon butter
1 tablespoon flour
4 cups beef stock
1 large raw potato, diced
¼ cup chopped celery
3 ounces tomatoes
1 whole clove
1 tablespoon chopped parsley
½ bay leaf
pinch thyme
3 peppercorns
salt and pepper to taste

Saute bacon, onions, and green pepper in butter. Add the flour to the above ingredients to make a roux. Stir to combine thoroughly. Add beef stock. Add potato, celery, and tomatoes. Bring to a boil. Place the spices in a cheesecloth bag and add to the pot. Simmer for 1 hour.

Remove the bag from the soup, skim off any foam and serve.

From: **The Golden Lamb Inn**
27 South Broadway
Lebanon

Laura's Potato Ham Soup

½ cup butter
1 cup chopped onion
4 cups mashed potatoes
1 quart milk
2 cups chopped ham
1 teaspoon salt
½ teaspoon pepper

In a saucepan, heat half of the butter over medium heat. Add the onions and saute until tender. Reduce the heat; add half of the milk and half of the potatoes. Stir well to blend. Gradually add the remaining milk and potatoes; stir in the ham, seasonings and remaining butter. Heat through but do not boil. Soup will thicken as it stands.

If using cold, leftover mashed potatoes, be sure to stir well before adding to the soup.

From: **The Inn at Honey Run**
6920 County Road 203
Millersburg

Grilled Red Pepper Soup

1 medium poblano pepper,
  finely diced
1½ bunches scallions, cleaned
  and sliced thin
5 shallots
5 tomatoes, peeled, seeded
  and diced
1 serrano pepper in adobo sauce,
  seeded and minced fine
⅓ cup olive oil
pinch dried basil
pinch dried thyme
1 gallon chicken stock
1 ounce fish sauce*
1 ounce rice wine vinegar*
1 tablespoon sugar

15 grilled peppers, red, yellow or
  chocolate, seeded, peeled
  and pureed
½ bunch basil, washed and
  shredded

*Note: Fish sauce and rice wine
vinegar may be obtained at Oriental specialty stores or in the
gourmet/specialty section of your
supermarket.

Prepare all the vegetables. In a heavy bottomed stockpot, heat the olive oil. Add and saute the poblano pepper, scallions and shallots over high heat until they begin to brown. Stir in the tomatoes and serrano pepper.

Add the herbs, chicken stock, fish sauce, rice wine vinegar and sugar. Bring to a boil, reduce the heat and simmer for about 15 minutes to develop the flavor.

Then add to the hot soup the pureed peppers and the ½ bunch basil which has been washed and shredded.

Garnish the soup with slices of yellow squash, grilled shrimp and more fresh basil.

From: **Sammy's**
1400 West 10th Street
Cleveland

Snowball Soup

5 ounces butter
6 ounces flour
1 quart chicken stock
2 ounces Madeira wine
1 pint heavy cream
1 teaspoon chopped pimentoes
1 teaspoon chopped fresh chives
24 snowballs
salt and pepper to taste

Snowballs:
6 ounces ground veal
¼ teaspoon nutmeg
1 egg white
2 ounces heavy cream
salt and pepper to taste

Make a roux with the flour and butter by mixing together. In a large stockpot, bring the chicken stock to a simmer, add the roux. Simmer for 30 minutes. While the soup is simmering, make the snowballs.

Puree the ground veal and nutmeg in a blender. Add the heavy cream in a slow drizzle. Add the egg white, salt, pepper and puree until ingredients are just mixed. Make each ball about ¼ ounce each.

In a saucepan, bring lightly salted water to a boil and poach the snowballs for a few minutes.

Strain the stock which has been simmmering. Add the Madeira and heavy cream and bring back to the boil. Add the snowballs, the pimentoes and serve. There should be 3 snowballs per serving. Sprinkle with the chopped chives, serve. Yield: 8 servings.

From: **The Chadwick Inn**
301 River Road
Maumee

Vintner's Pot

This is a hearty soup made during the annual grape crush for workers and their families.

1 pound bulk country
  pork sausage
1 clove garlic, chopped
1 medium onion, chopped
4 medium carrots, peeled and
  chopped
3 ribs celery, chopped
1 teaspoon crushed red pepper
1 cup chopped green cabbage
2 turnips, peeled and chopped
2 potatoes, chopped
1 bay leaf
1 teaspoon dried thyme
1 teaspoon caraway seed
Chicken stock or water to cover

Slowly brown sausage in a large stockpot, using a spoon to break apart. Set aside cooked sausage, reserving the fat in the pot.

Saute the garlic, onion, carrots, celery, and crushed red pepper in the fat. Add the cabbage, turnips, potatoes and seasonings. Cover with the stock or water and simmer slowly until all the ingredients are tender. Pay attention to the liquid, being sure that it covers the ingredients and the heat is low.

When soup is done, return the sausage to the pot. In addition, ground up ham scraps may be added for additional flavor.

From: **Arnold's Bar & Grill**
210 East Eighth Street
Cincinnati

Meat & Poultry

Meat and Poultry

When asked to submit recipes, restaurant chefs seem to favor the meat and poultry category above all others, even dessert. Whether this is because they feel certain people will order an entree, when they might skip soup, or salad, or dessert or whether they just feel the category offers more scope for their talents, is unclear.

What is clear is that there are many wonderful recipes to try here, many new ways to cook old favorites and a good share of ethnic recipes as well. If you're tired of the same old thing, you've turned to the right chapter. These should perk up your weary palate. Read on, cook on and enjoy!

Chicken Bleu Cheese

½ cup heavy cream
2 cups fresh bleu cheese,
  crumbled
1 tablespoon cornstarch
4 tablespoons water
2 tablespoons red wine
½ cup butter
6 8-ounce boneless
  chicken breasts
seasoned egg wash*
seasoned flour*
24 spears of white asparagus
  (green may be substituted)
12 pieces crispy bacon

*Seasoned egg wash:
6 eggs
1 teaspoon granulated garlic
1 teaspoon white pepper
1 tablespoon Worcestershire
  sauce

Seasoned flour:
2 cups flour
1 tablespoon granulated garlic
1 teaspoon white pepper
2 teaspoons paprika
1 teaspooon salt

Pour the heavy cream into a heavy bottomed saucepan and heat over medium heat until hot, but do not boil. When the cream is hot, stir in half the crumbled bleu cheese and cook until the cheese is melted, stirring occasionally. Add the remaining bleu cheese and repeat the process until all the cheese is melted. Mix the cornstarch with the water and add into the bleu cheese, heavy cream mixture. Cook for 4 minutes over medium heat, stirring occasionally. Add the red wine and set the sauce aside, keeping warm.

Melt the butter in a saute pan until it is hot. Dip the chicken into the egg wash, then into the seasoned flour and saute in the melted butter until golden brown on each side. If using the white asparagus, saute quickly in the hot butter. If using green asparagus, blanch in boiling water for 4 minutes. Place a chicken breast on plate, top with 4 spears of asparagus, and nap sauce over the breast. Garnish with the crispy bacon crumbled on top.

From: **The Gun Room
at the Lafayette Hotel**
101 Front Street
Marietta

Chicken with Ginger

4 tablespoons peanut oil
4 tablespoons chopped onion
1 teaspoon chopped garlic
1½ chicken breasts, boned and skinned
4 tablespoons nuoe mam (fish sauce*)
2 teaspoons caramel
2 tablespoons sugar
1 cup hot water
½ cup green onions, sliced
2 tablespoons shredded fresh ginger
½ teaspoon cornstarch
4 tablespoons cold water
*Noue mam or Vietnamese fish sauce should be available in Oriental groceries, specialty stores or the gourmet section of your supermarket.

Heat a saute pan and add the oil. When hot, add the chopped onion, garlic and chicken, cut in strips. Stir fry until the onions are golden, add the fish sauce, caramel, and sugar. Stir until bubbling, then pour in hot water. Cook until mixture thickens slightly. Add the green onions and ginger and cook until the onions are partially cooked. Mix the cornstarch with the cold water and add to the pan. Stir quickly to thicken slightly. Garnish with crushed peanuts sprinkled on top of the chicken, serve with white rice.

From: **Minh Anh Restaurant**
5428 Detroit Avenue
Cleveland

Charbroiled Marinated Chicken Breasts

3 whole breasts of chicken

Lime Basil Marinade:
1 cup vegetable oil
⅓ cup fresh lime juice
1 teaspoon basil
1 teaspoon parsley
¾ teaspoon salt
⅛ teaspoon black pepper
3 cloves garlic, minced
3 drops Louisiana-style hot
* pepper sauce*
½ teaspoon sugar

Combine all ingredients for the marinade in a bowl, mix thoroughly. Allow marinade to stand at room temperature for 15 minutes. At this time, clean, rinse and split chicken breasts in half. Place the marinade in a large glass bowl, add the chicken and mix well so all of the marinade is evenly distributed over chicken.

Cover well. Place in refrigerator for 24-48 hours before charbroiling over open coals.

To bake, preheat oven to 350 degrees. On the top of stove, in an oven proof pan, brown the chicken on the outside quickly and place in the oven for 45 minutes. Baste with butter for a rich flavor. Yield: 6 servings.

From: **The Bryn Mawr
Restaurant**
3758 Lancaster Road
Granville

Grilled Breast of Chicken
with Fresh Basil Tomato Sauce

4 chicken breasts,
   boned and halved
3 garlic cloves
16 large, fresh basil leaves

Marinade:
½ cup white wine vinegar
5 tablespoons olive oil
½ teaspoon salt
¼ teaspoon pepper
1½ teaspoons minced garlic

Tomato Basil Sauce:
¼ cup chopped onion
¼ cup chopped green pepper
½ teaspoon minced garlic
2 tablespoons butter
2 8-ounce cans tomato sauce
½ teaspoon salt
¼ teaspoon pepper
½ cup chopped fresh basil leaves

Slide ⅛ of the minced garlic and two fresh basil leaves under the skin of each chicken breast. Place breasts in a non-reactive pan. Combine the marinade ingredients and pour over the chicken breasts. Marinate 4-6 hours or overnight.

Remove chicken breasts from marinade. Grill over hot coals 8-10 minutes on each side. Serve with the Tomato Basil Sauce.

To prepare sauce, saute the onion, green pepper, and garlic in the butter until the onion is tender. Stir in tomato sauce. Add the salt and pepper. Simmer for 10 minutes. Add the chopped basil right before serving. Yield: 8 servings.

From: **The Heritage
Restaurant**
7664 Wooster Pike
Cincinnati

Grilled Fresh Chicken Breast
with Lobster Claw Bearnaise

8 8-ounce boneless
   chicken breasts
8 servings creamed spinach*
8 ounces lobster claw and
   knuckle meat
bearnaise sauce

Bearnaise sauce:
8 egg yolks
1½ pounds unsalted butter
juice of 1 lemon
2 teaspoons salt
1 teaspoon white pepper
1 ounce fresh tarragon
3 ounces tarragon vinegar

*See recipe for creamed spinach
in the chapter on vegetables.

Skin the chicken breasts and trim the fat off. Place top side down on grill, then rotate to make crisscross marks. Turn and grill on other side until done, 8-10 minutes.

Place 4 ounces of the creamed spinach on each plate, place a chicken breast on top of each helping of spinach. Arrange some of the lobster meat on each chicken breast and top with the bearnaise sauce.

For the bearnaise sauce, after separating the eggs, heat the butter on low heat until it has separated. The cream will fall to the bottom.

Place the eggs in a food processor with a rubber blade. Turn on high speed. Using a ladle, skim off the oil of the butter, being careful not to get any of the cream. Add this slowly in a thin stream to the eggs. Process until the eggs and butter have reached the consistency of a thick pudding. On pulse, add the lemon juice, salt and pepper. Then add the tarragon and vinegar. Process until the sauce is smooth and has a creamy consistency. Place in a container and store at room temperature until ready to use.

Garnish with sprigs of fresh parsley and serve. Yield: 8 servings.

From: **Chester's Road House**
9678 Montgomery Road
Montgomery

Grilled Chicken with Proscuitto and Basil

2 pounds chicken breasts,
  boned and skinned
16 slices proscuitto, thinly sliced
16 leaves fresh basil
2-3 cups good Italian dressing
4-6 wooden skewers

Cut chicken into 16 equal strips. (Any left over chicken pieces may be used for chicken salad.) Lay out the 16 slices of proscuitto on work surface. Top each slice of proscuitto with a fresh basil leaf, then place a strip of chicken over each proscuitto-basil stack. Roll each stack, making sure the proscuitto is on the outside. Place 4 on a skewer and marinate in a good Italian dressing, preferably homemade. Marinate for at least 2 hours. Place on a hot grill and cook, turning and basting for approximately 10 minutes. Serve with a fresh tossed salad and lightly seasoned angel hair pasta (capellini). Yield: 4 servings.

From: **The Watermark Restaurant**
1250 Old River Road
Cleveland

Quails with Fresh Pineapple and Curaçao
Salmis de Cailles aux Ananas

1 large, ripe pineapple
8 quails
butter
salt and pepper
2 ounces diced carrots
2 ounces diced celery
2 ounces diced onions
½ pound quartered mushrooms
1 sprig thyme
1 bay leaf
6 ounces dry white wine
3 ounces Madeira
3 ounces Curacao
1 cup veal stock
1½ ounces unsalted butter

Cut off both ends of the pineapple. Cut the pineapple into 4 equal slices. With a melon ball cutter, hollow out each quarter of the pineapple without piercing the bottom. Reserve the pineapple balls and the juice.

Cut the quails in 2, remove the back bones. Reserve the back bones, necks, giblets and liver to add to the sauce.

Season the quail with salt and pepper. Saute them in butter, browning them. Remove the quails. Add the vegetables, thyme and bay leaf, cook for 5 minutes. Remove the excess butter. Place the quail back in the skillet. Deglaze the pan with the wine, Madeira and half of the Curacao. Add the pineapple juice and veal stock and bring to a boil. Cover the skillet and cook in a 375 degree oven for 15 minutes. Remove the quail, place them in the pineapple quarters. Add the pineapple balls, keeping hot. Reduce the sauce and strain through a fine strainer. Thicken the sauce with the unsalted butter. Do not boil. Add the rest of the Curacao. Pour the sauce on the quail and serve. Yield: 4 servings.

From: **La Maisonette**
114 East Sixth Street
Cincinnati

Steak au Poivre

2 tablespoons melted butter
4 tablespoons coarsely chopped
    whole peppercorns
4 10- to 12-ounce NY strip steaks
2 ounces brandy
2 cups veal or beef stock
2 cups crème fraîche

Place the two tablespoons of melted butter in a large platter and coat the steaks with the butter. Press the chopped peppercorns to both sides of the buttered steaks.

Heat skillet until it's very hot. Cook the steaks 3 minutes on each side for rare, 5 minutes for medium rare.

Add brandy and flambe the steaks. The flame will get very high, make sure your face is out of the flame's reach. Remove them from the skillet and keep warm.

To the same skillet, add veal stock, reduce the sauce in half. Add crème fraîche, reduce again until the sauce is thick enough to coat a spoon. Make sure you scrape the bottom of the skillet and serve over the steaks.

From: **Lock 24 Restaurant**
State Route 154
Elkton

Tournedos of Beef
in Madeira Sauce

1½ ounces Madeira
1 ounce chopped shallots
1 ounce chanterelles mushrooms
1 ounce sun-dried tomatoes,
    remoistened
1½ ounces veal demiglace*
1 ounce butter
8 ounces beef tenderloin,
    cut into 2 medallions

*Demiglace is stock that has been
reduced to a sauce consistency.

In a heavy bottomed saucepan, mix the wine and the shallots and reduce the liquid by half. Then add the mushrooms, tomatoes, and demiglace stock and reduce again by half, or until the sauce thickens.

Put the butter in a very hot skillet and cook meat to the desired degree of doneness. Place on warmed plate, nap with sauce. Serve, garnished with fresh watercress. Yield: 1 serving.

From:

The Fig Tree
909 Vine Street
Cincinnati

Tournedos Baltimore

2 3-ounce beef filets
3 tablespoons melted butter
2 tablespoons diced onion
1 tablespoon diced green pepper
3 slices tomato
5 ounces brown sauce
dash of brandy
dash of Worcestershire
   sauce

Saute the filets in the butter. Add the onions, green pepper and tomatoes. After the meat is cooked to the desired degree of doneness, add the brandy, brown sauce and Worcestershire sauce. Season to taste, garnish and serve. Yield: 1 serving.

From: **Ricardo's**
Owens-Illinois Building
One Seagate, Park Level 118
Toledo

Tournedos Dumas

Onion Sauce:
1 cup chopped onions
1¼ cups milk
2 tablespoons butter
2 tablespoons flour
salt and pepper to taste

4 4-ounce beef filets
4 toast rounds
4 slices ham
2 ounces grated Gruyère cheese

Prepare the onion sauce by simmering the onions in the milk. Heat the butter in a saute pan and stir in flour. Cook for a minute. Add onion and milk; cook until thickened. Salt and pepper to taste.

Broil filets or pan fry to degree of doneness desired. Place on toast rounds, top with onion sauce, ham and grated cheese. Broil to melt cheese. Yield: 2 servings.

From: **Peerless Mill Inn**
319 South Second Street
Miamisburg

Roast Lamb
with Veal Mousseline

2 cloves garlic
1 shallot
4 teaspoons rosemary
8 cups spinach
2 pounds veal stew meat
1-2 cups heavy cream
1 boneless lamb loin
3 pounds caul fat
salt and pepper

In a food processor, chop the garlic, shallots, rosemary and spinach, which you have washed, de-stemmed and dried. Add the veal and the cream until a smooth, thick consistency is reached.

Preheat oven to 450 degrees. Take the boneless lamb loin, which you have had your butcher bone for you, and cut it in half across the grain.

The caul fat, which you have obtained from your butcher, should be washed and treated as you would a natural sausage casing. Keep it submerged in the water until you use it.

Lay the caul fat flat on a table or work surface. Take the mousseline and completely coat the lamb loin to a depth of 1/8 to 1/4 inch until the loin is completely encased. Roll this in the fat, the caul fat will keep the lamb loin intact.

Saute the lamb in hot vegetable oil for five minutes on each side. Then bake for a half hour to 45 minutes in the oven.

Serve this with a lamb reduction sauce which you make by browning the lamb bones

from the loin in the oven, then putting in a stockpot with water to cover and boiling down until you have a lamb demiglace.

Take two cups cabernet sauvignon and a sprig of rosemary, reduce the wine to ⅛ cup and add the lamb demiglace. Reduce to desired flavor and serve with the lamb loin.

From: **The Baricelli Inn**
2203 Cornell Road
Cleveland

Braised Lamb Shanks
The Golden Lamb

4 lamb shanks, approx.
  1 pound each
3 tablespoons vegetable
  shortening
1 large onion, diced
1 cup fresh mushrooms, quartered
¾ cup diced celery
1 turnip, peeled and diced
3 tablespoons tomato paste
salt and pepper to taste
5 tablespoons flour
¼ teaspoon black pepper
2 cloves garlic, minced
⅛ teaspoon rosemary leaves,
  finely chopped
1 pinch thyme
1 bay leaf
½ cup Burgundy
6 cups good lamb stock or
  beef stock

Season the lamb shanks with salt and pepper. Heat the shortening in a heavy roaster or braiser. Brown the lamb shanks on all sides. Add the onions, mushrooms, celery and turnips. Brown.

Add the tomato paste and mix in thoroughly with the juices. Sprinkle the flour on the meat and brown lightly. Add the garlic, rosemary, thyme, and bay leaf. Add the Burgundy and the lamb stock. Cover the roaster/braiser and braise the lamb shanks in a 350-degree oven for 1-1½ hours or until done.

Skim off the fat occasionally. Taste and add salt and pepper, if necessary. Arrange the lamb shanks on plate, cover with the sauce and sprinkle with fresh, chopped parsley.

From: **The Golden Lamb**
         227 South Broadway
         Lebanon

Apple Stuffed Pork Loin

5 pound boneless pork roast
2 cups apple cider

Stuffing:
5 cups good bread cubes
1 cup chopped celery
1 cup chopped onions
6 apples, Melrose, if possible
1½ cups chicken broth
dried basil to taste
poultry seasoning to taste
salt and pepper to taste
4 eggs, beaten

Place boneless pork roast in a shallow roasting pan. Pour apple cider over pork, cover and bake in a 350-degree oven for about 2 hours, until tender.

While pork cooks, prepare the stuffing. Place the bread cubes in a large bowl and set aside.

Saute the celery, onions and apples, which you have cored and chopped, in a little butter. Pour over the bread cubes, then add the chicken broth. Mix until well blended. Add the seasonings to suit your own taste, let cool. Add the eggs to make the stuffing moist. Place in a baking pan and heat until warmed through.

Make gravy from the pan drippings, by whisking in a little flour and adding chicken broth as needed.

To serve spoon out stuffing onto plate. Slice thin slices of pork and lay on top of stuffing. Ladle gravy over the top and serve. Garnish with fresh apple slices, or spiced crabapples and watercress. Yield: 6-8 servings.

From: **The Apple Farm Restaurant**
262 Pearl Road
Brunswick

Roasted Pork Medallions
with Watercress Sauce

12 pork tenderloin medallions
¼ cup dry white wine
¼ cup butter
¼ cup finely diced onion
¼ cup flour
1 cup heavy cream
1 cup half & half cream
¾ teaspoon salt
⅛ teaspoon pepper

½ cup chopped watercress leaves
peanut oil
salt
pepper
flour

Have your butcher cut the pork medallions so they are the same size.

Place wine and butter in a heavy bottomed 1-quart saucepan. Heat until boiling. Add the onions and cook until the onions turn clear. Remove the pan from the heat, add the flour and whisk well until all the butter is absorbed into the flour. Add the creams, season with the salt and pepper and whisk briskly until the mixture returns to the boil. Add the watercress and remove from the heat. Keep warm.

In a large saute or frying pan, place a little peanut oil and heat until very hot. Season the meat with salt and pepper and dredge in flour, shaking off the excess. Place the floured and seasoned medallions in the pan and brown quickly on both sides. Be sure the medallions are cooked through. Transfer to a warm serving platter, cover with the sauce, garnish with vegetables, potatoes, or rice and top with fresh watercress sprigs. Yield: 12 servings.

To improve the sauce, after the meat has been removed, add ½ cup of wine to the saute or frying pan and whisk, deglazing, just until the wine boils. Strain the wine from the pan into the sauce, whisk to integrate the deglazing liquid into the sauce and pour over the meat.

From: **The Bryn Mawr
Restaurant**
3758 Lancaster Road
Granville

Veal Birds

2 veal scallops, 6-8 ounces total
4 ounces crabmeat
salt and pepper to taste
flour
1-3 tablespoons melted butter
1 tablespoon fresh lemon juice
2 tablespoons white wine

Pound the veal thin. Wrap the crabmeat, which you have picked over to be sure there are no membranes or bits of shell in it, in the veal slices and secure with butcher string or toothpicks. Salt and pepper the veal "birds" and dredge in flour.

In a heavy bottomed saute pan, melt the butter until it is hot and foaming but not smoking. Put the veal in the pan and cook until browned on all sides. Add the lemon juice and the wine. Just before serving add 1 tablespoon solid butter, whisking in briskly to finish the sauce. Serve over rice. Yield: 1 serving.

From: **Ricardo's**
Owens-Illinois Building
One Seagate, Park Level 118
Toledo

Medallions of Veal with Morels

1 7-8 pound veal loin,
  boned, cut into medallions
4 ounces clarified butter
2 shallots, minced
2 ounces dried morels
½ cup dry white wine
1 cup demiglace
1 cup heavy cream
salt and pepper to taste

Debone the veal loin and remove all fat, cutting into 6 ½-inch medallions, or have your butcher do it. Put butter in heavy bottomed skillet or saute pan and heat. Saute the medallions for one minute on both sides. The veal medallions should be light golden brown when removed from the pan. Add the minced shallots to the pan and cook until golden brown.

Add the morels, which you have soaked in water according to directions, adding the white wine as well. Reduce, then add the demiglace and reduce until the sauce thickens. Finish with heavy cream and reduce until the sauce has the required (desired) thickness. Place the veal medallions on a serving platter and pour morel sauce over the veal. Garnish with vegetables or pasta.

From: **L'Auberge**
4120 Far Hills Avenue
Dayton

Ris de Veau au Calvados

24 ounces veal sweetbreads,
trimmed and parboiled
24 wedges of apple, peeled
6 teaspoons finely diced
carrots
6 teaspoons finely diced celery
3 teaspoons chopped truffles
6 teaspoons finely diced
white of leek
3 teaspoons chopped shallots
3 ounces calvados
8 ounces heavy cream
flour, butter, salt and pepper

Flour the sweetbreads lightly. Season with salt and pepper. Saute in butter, brown on all sides, remove, keep warm. In the same skillet, add the apple wedges, all the diced vegetables, and truffles. Add a little butter if necessary, stir and do not let brown. Deglaze with the calvados, then add the cream. Cook and reduce until the sauce thickens slightly. Check the seasoning. Put the sweetbreads on warmed platter. Pour sauce on the sweetbreads. Sprinkle with fresh chopped parsley. Serve with potato and a green vegetable.

From: **La Maisonette**
            114 East Sixth Street
            Cincinnati

Veal Romano

6 4-ounce veal cutlets
½ cup olive oil
½ cup freshly grated
   Romano cheese
16 ounces capellini
(angel hair pasta)
18 sun-dried tomatoes
seasoned flour*
seasoned egg wash*
Vinaigrette*

*Seasoned flour:
2 cups flour
1 tablespoon granulated garlic
1 tablespoon onion powder
1 teaspoon white pepper
1 teaspoon basil
1 teaspoon oregano

*Seasoned egg wash:
5 eggs
1 teaspoon granulated garlic
1 tablespoon Worcestershire
   sauce
¼ cup freshly grated
   Romano cheese
¼ cup milk

Bring 4 quarts of water to a boil. Add ¼ cup of the olive oil and a tablespoon of salt. Add the capellini noodles. Cook, stirring occasionally. Drain pasta and cool in cold water. Cut the veal into medallions and pound thin with a meat mallet (you can use a rolling pin, if you have one of the heavy smooth European ones). Heat the remaining ¼ cup olive oil in a saute pan over medium heat; dredge the veal medallions in seasoned flour, then in the seasoned egg wash, making sure that the Romano cheese from the egg wash gets onto the veal; then saute in olive oil until golden brown on both sides. Remove the veal from the saute pan, turn heat to low and add sun-dried tomatoes. Mix vinaigrette and capellini in a heavy saucepan and cook over medium heat until hot. Place capellini on plate and arrange 1 veal medallion, 1 sun-dried tomato, 1 veal medallion, etc. (using 4 veal medallions and 3 sun-dried tomatoes per serving). Top veal with remaining ¼ cup of Romano cheese. Serve immediately. Yield: 6 servings.

*Vinaigrette:

*1 cup extra-virgin
olive oil
½ cup cider vinegar
3 cloves garlic, minced
2 tablespoons chopped
    scallions
1 teaspoon basil
½ teaspoon oregano
1 tablespoon diced red pimentoes
1 dash Worcestershire
    sauce
⅛ teaspoon white pepper*

From: **The Gun Room
at the Lafayette Hotel**
101 Front Street
Marietta

Veal Scallops with Eggplant and Fresh Tomatoes
Scalloppine di Vitello de Lorenzo

4 ¼-inch slices eggplant, skinned
3 ounces clarified margarine
3 ounces olive oil
6 2-ounce veal scallops,
    sliced ¼ inch and pounded thin
6 tablespoons flour
½ ounce diced shallots
3 ounces thinly sliced
    mushrooms
2 very thin slices proscuitto
1 large tomato, peeled,
    seeded and julienned
⅛ teaspoon fines herbes
2 ounces Madeira
5 ounces espagnole sauce
2 ounces unsalted butter

salt and pepper to taste
1 tablespoon chopped parsley

*espagnole sauce is a lightly
thickened brown sauce not quite
as thick as a demiglace, made
from meat stock.

Salt and weigh down eggplant slices for 1 hour. Pat dry and flour the eggplant. Heat 1 ounce each of the clarified margarine and olive oil until a light haze forms over it. Add the dusted eggplant and brown on each side. Remove from skillet and keep warm.

Heat the remaining margarine and olive oil in a large skillet, again until a light haze forms over it. Lightly flour the veal, place in the skillet, season with salt and pepper, and lightly brown on one side. Turn them and degrease the skillet, removing the excess oil. Add the shallots, mushrooms, proscuitto, fresh tomatoes, fines herbes and saute for two minutes. Add the Madeira over high flame and deglaze. Add the espagnole sauce and fresh butter and cook until butter is incorporated in the sauce; adjust the seasoning.

Place the warmed eggplant on each service plate and layer veal over it. Place the remaining tomatoes and mushrooms over the veal scallops and pour remaining sauce over it, garnish with chopped parsley and serve. Yield: 2 servings.

From: **Ristorante Giovanni**
25550 Chagrin Boulevard
Cleveland

Fish & Seafood

Fish and Seafood

Despite the news that beef is making a comeback in popularity and that game is the new excitement in entrees, fish and seafood remain popular with many of us.

Through the creativity of many chefs we have learned to love fish and seafood and will not soon give it up. Fortunately, many chefs continue to devise new and exciting ways of preparing the bounty of rivers, lakes and ocean. Some of the recipes are simple, elegant and delicious. Some are more complicated, almost as wonderful to look at as they are to consume.

Here are fish and seafood as prepared by Ohio's finest chefs.

Fillet of Brill
with Fines Herbes Sauce

2 pounds of brill fillet
½ pound pike fillet
6 ounces raw lobster meat
6 ounces bay shrimp
2 ounces truffles
2 pints heavy cream
2 pounds puff pastry dough

Stock and Sauce:
2 tablespoons fresh parsley
1 tablespoon chives
½ tablespoon fresh tarragon
4 ounces unsalted butter
6 ounces onions
6 ounces carrots
6 ounces celery
1 bay leaf
1 pinch of thyme
1 quart of dry white wine

Season the fillets with salt and pepper and set aside.

Put the pike, lobster, shrimp and truffles in the blender or food processor. Puree, then transfer to a large bowl. Season with salt and pepper. Add 1 pint of the heavy cream and mix well. Spread the preparation evenly on the fillet of brill.

Preheat oven to 375 degrees. Roll the puff pastry ¼-inch thick. Lay the fillets of fish on top and cut the dough around it in the shape of a fish. Cut the rest of the dough in a fish shape 2 inches larger so it can overlap the bottom part easily.

Decorate with the edge of a knife, imitating the fish scales, fins and head.

Brush with an egg wash made from 2 egg yolks thinned with a little cold water.

Cook in oven for 20 minutes, until golden brown, serve with Fines Herbes Sauce.

For the sauce: In a heavy saucepan, melt the 4 tablespoons butter, saute the bones and skins of the fish, the minced onions, celery and carrots with the thyme and bay leaf. Do not brown. Cover with the dry white wine and 1 quart of water.

Bring to a boil, season with salt and pepper. Simmer for at least 1 hour, strain through a fine strainer, then reduce to 2 cups if necessary.

Add to the reduced stock the other pint of heavy cream and reduce to 1½ cups, correcting seasoning.

Before serving, add fresh chopped parsley, fresh chopped chives and fresh chopped tarragon, if available. Serve with fillets of brill. Yield: 6 servings

From: **La Maisonette**
114 East Sixth Street
Cincinnati

Maryland Crab Cakes
with Chester's Road House Mustard Sauce

Crab Cakes:
1 medium green pepper
2 ounces fresh parsley
1 cup good mayonnaise
1 tablespoon dry mustard
5 eggs
1 dash Tabasco sauce
1 teaspoon white pepper
2 cups fresh bread crumbs
½ pound red crabmeat

Clean the green pepper and parsley and chop fine. Place in a large bowl. Add mayonnaise, mustard, eggs, Tabasco and white pepper and mix until thoroughly blended. Add the bread crumbs and crabmeat and mix until the bread has become moist. Place in refrigerator until chilled through.

Mustard Sauce:

1 cup good mayonnaise
2 teaspoons Worcestershire
* sauce*
2 tablespoons Dijon-style
* mustard*
1 teaspoon white pepper
¼ cup half & half cream

Place all ingredients into a small bowl and whip at high speed until thoroughly combined. Place in a non-reactive container and refrigerate until ready to use.

Make 8 5-ounce patties out of the crab cake mixture. Heat 3 ounces cooking oil in a large skillet. Turn the heat down to medium low. Carefully place the crab cakes in the skillet, being careful not to splash the oil. Brown on both sides and blot dry on paper towels before placing on the plate. Put the mustard sauce to one side of the crab cakes and garnish with parsley. Serve. Yield: 8 servings.

From: **Chester's Road House**
9678 Montgomery Road
Montgomery

Linguini de la Mar

2 pounds linguini
½ pound shrimp, peeled and
   deveined
½ pound scallops
1 cup chopped clams and juice
1 ounce clarified butter
½ cup chablis or other white wine
juice of 1 lemon
4 ounces unsalted butter,
   softened
½ teaspoon basil
½ teaspoon thyme
½ teaspoon oregano
1½ teaspoon chopped garlic
1 teaspoon salt
½ teaspoon white pepper
1½ cups chopped tomatoes

In a large heavy saucepan, bring water to a rolling boil. Put in drop of oil and salt. Add linguini, cook al dente.

In a large skillet, melt the clarified butter, add the scallops, shrimp and clams, reserving the clam juice. Cook just until the scallops lose their translucence. Add the chablis, lemon juice and clam juice and reduce by half. Then add the softened butter, bit by bit, beating in each addition to make the sauce. Add the herbs, garlic and salt and pepper. Add the tomatoes.

Drain the linguini thoroughly and toss with the seafood mixture thoroughly. Serve with a loaf of good, crusty French bread. Yield: 4-6 servings.

From: **The Fig Tree**
907 Vine Street
Cincinnati

Panizotti of Scallops and Shrimp over Cabbage with Walnut Sauce
Panizotti di Mare con Salsa di Noche

Pasta dough:
1½ cups flour
3 eggs
½ teaspoon salt

Filling:
3 tablespoons minced shallots
½ cup sliced fresh shitake
   mushrooms
2 tablespoons butter
2 tablespoons dry white wine
⅛ teaspoon cayenne
½ teaspoon salt
pepper to taste
½ cup whipping cream
4 ounces peeled and deveined
   shrimp, coarsely chopped
1 egg, for sealing squares
5 ounces sea scallops
3 ounces boned halibut

Sauce:
6 tablespoons butter
1⅔ cups heavy cream
¾ cup freshly grated Parmesan
cheese
¼ teaspoon ground nutmeg
pepper to taste
5 tablespoons finely
   chopped walnuts
5 egg yolks*

Put the flour, eggs and salt into a food processor and process until it forms a smooth dough. Form into a ball, wrap it in plastic wrap and place in the refrigerator for 30 minutes.

To make the filling, saute the shallots and mushrooms in the butter until limp, about 3 minutes. Add the white wine and cook another 3 minutes. Cool slightly and put into the bowl of a food processor equipped with a knife blade. Add the scallops, halibut, cayenne, salt and pepper. Process until blended but not pureed. With the processor running, add the cream in a steady stream until the mixture is the consistency of heavy pudding. Place in a mixing bowl and fold in the chopped shrimp.

Roll out the pasta on a lightly floured surface or put through a pasta machine, and cut into 3½-inch squares. Place a slightly rounded tablespoon of the filling in the center of each square. Moisten the outside edge with the egg and lift the corners toward center, forming a point. Then completely seal the edges by pinching them lightly. Cook the panizotti squares in salted boiling water for 4 or 5 minutes. Lift out with a slotted spoon and drain.

To make the sauce, beat the butter and heavy cream in a saucepan over medium heat until bubbling. Remove from the heat.

Base:

¼ *pound minced bacon*
½ *head Savoy cabbage, cored*
and cut into thin strips
salt and pepper to taste

Add cheese, nutmeg and pepper, stir until cheese is melted. Add the chopped walnuts, then add the egg yolks and immediately whisk to avoid curdling. (See note*).

To cook the base, saute the bacon until crisp and then add the cabbage and cook just until limp.

To serve, divide the cabbage among 4 plates (or 8 when used as first course) as a bed for the pasta squares. Place approximately 8 panizotti squares atop the cabbage, apply a light portion of the sauce and sprinkle chopped walnuts atop as a garnish. Yield: 4 entree size servings or 8 appetizer servings.

*Note: The egg yolks make a richer, slightly thicker sauce, but the addition of the yolks makes it difficult to reheat the sauce, so although Giovanni's cooks are adept with such sauces, we recommend leaving them out so it can be made earlier and reheated just before serving. The thinner sauce is quite pleasant with the other rich ingredients.

From: **Ristorante Giovanni**
25550 Chagrin Boulevard
Beachwood

Salmon with Tarragon Cream Sauce

Saumon a la Creme Estragon

6 salmon steaks

Court Bouillon:
1 rib celery, cut in 3-inch lengths
½ onion
1 bay leaf
2 tablespoons white vinegar
2 quarts water
1 cup dry white wine

Tarragon Cream Sauce:
1 tablespoon butter
2 teaspoons chopped shallots
2 cloves garlic, chopped
½ cup white wine
1 tablespoon dry tarragon
   or 2 tablespoons fresh
2 cups heavy cream
1 whole tomato, peeled,
   seeded and diced

salt and pepper to taste

Put all the ingredients for the court bouillon in a shallow pan large enough to hold all 6 of the salmon steaks. Bring the bouillon to a simmer and put the fish in. Poach for 12-15 minutes. When the fish are done, remove from the liquid with a spatula. Remove the outer skin and the center bone from the steaks. The other bones should slide right out also.

In a medium non-reactive saucepan, place the butter and brown the shallots and garlic. Add the white wine and tarragon and reduce by ¾. Add the heavy cream and tomato. Salt and pepper to taste. Nap the sauce over the fish and serve. Yield: 6 servings.

From: **L'Armagnac
Restaurant Francais**
121 South Sixth Street
Columbus

Scallops Florentine

3 tablespoons butter
1 tablespoon fresh dill
juice of ½ lemon
8 ounces sea scallops
¼ cup white wine
½ cup heavy cream
fresh spinach
provolone cheese

Heat the butter, dill, and lemon juice in a medium skillet. Add the scallops and cook lightly.

Place scallops on bed of spinach, which has been washed, dried and stems removed. Top with provolone cheese and place under broiler until cheese is melted. Pour off liquid in bottom of pan.

In another pan reduce the wine by half. Add the heavy cream to the reduced wine and simmer until thickened. Pour thickened sauce over the cheese, scallop, and spinach mixture. Serve. Yield: 2 servings.

From: **The Garden at the Lighthouse**
226 East Perry Street
Port Clinton

Shrimp and Scallops
in Champagne Sauce

3 tablespoons clarified butter
1 pound shrimp, shelled
*   and deveined*
1 pound sea scallops
8 ounces dry champagne
1½ cups crème fraîche*
⅓ cup finely julienned carrot
⅓ cup finely julienned zucchini
⅓ cup finely julienned yellow
*   squash*
salt and pepper to taste

Heat a large skillet, add the clarified butter. When the butter is hot and foaming, add the shrimp and the scallops. Cook until almost done, 3-4 minutes. They will finish cooking in the sauce.

Add the champagne and stir well. Using a slotted spoon, transfer the shrimp and scallops to a heated platter. Boil the champagne/butter mixture down to half. Add the crème fraîche and reduce again until the sauce thickens slightly, about 8-10 minutes. It will

crème fraîche may be made by adding one teaspoonful of yogurt to heavy cream and allow it to sit out overnight.

coat the spoon. Add the julienne vegetables, put the shrimp and scallops back in the sauce. Season with salt and pepper. Serve hot. Yield: 4-6 servings.

From: **Lock 24 Restaurant**
State Route 154
Elkton

Shrimp Frangelico

36 large shrimp
4 ounces unsalted hazelnuts
1½ ounces Frangelico or
any hazelnut liqueur
4 ounces butter
16 ounces saffron pasta*
6 ounces thinly sliced
Brie cheese

*Note: Saffron pasta is available in most gourmet food stores and in the gourmet section of some supermarkets.

Peel and devein shrimp and set aside. Bring 4 quarts of water, 2 ounces of butter and 1 teaspoon salt to a rapid boil, add saffron pasta and cook al dente. Rinse pasta in cold water and set aside. Place hazelnuts in food processor or blender and grind coarsely. Place hazelnuts on a cookie sheet and roast in a 400-degree oven until light golden brown, remove from oven and cool. Melt butter in saute pan over medium heat until hot, add shrimp and roasted hazelnuts and saute until the shrimp are done. Heat pasta in hot water. Add Frangelico liqueur to shrimp and hazelnuts in pan, tilting pan to ignite, cook until flame is gone. Drain pasta and arrange on plate. Place 6 shrimp on the bed of pasta and spoon hazelnut mixture over shrimp. Top shrimp with thinly sliced Brie and melt in 400-degree oven. Serve immediately. Yield: 6 servings.

From: **The Lafayette**
101 Front Street
Marietta

Turban of Sole Saumonette

3 pounds fresh sole
1 pound salmon
3 egg whites
4 cups heavy cream
1 cup white wine
salt and pepper to taste
butter
2 ounces minced shallots
pinch cayenne pepper
pinch nutmeg

Fillet the sole and make a stock with the bones.

Mince salmon in the food processor, season with salt and pepper to taste, add nutmeg and cayenne. Add the 3 egg whites to the mixture and process. Rest the mixture for 2 hours in the refrigerator. Add 2 cups of the cream slowly so the mixture does not break.

Flatten the sole fillets and spread salmon mousse ½-inch thick on the fish. Roll each piece up and place them in a well buttered pan. Add the minced shallots, the white wine and 2 cups of the fish stock which you have made from the bones of the sole. Poach the fish fillets gently for 6 minutes. Remove them from the pan and keep warm. Reduce the liquid by boiling over a high heat. Add the remaining 2 cups of heavy cream and reduce until the sauce thickens. Place the stuffed sole fillets on a serving dish and pour the sauce over them. Garnish with vegetables, parsley and fleurons. Yield: 6 servings.

From: **L'Auberge**
4120 Far Hills Avenue
Dayton

Bag Baked Walleye

Parchment paper
1 walleye fillet
2 mushrooms
½ red pepper
1 rib celery
1 small carrot
juice of ½ lemon
dash salt and pepper
½ ounce baby shrimp
¼ cup heavy cream

Preheat oven to 350 degrees. Place the walleye fillet on the center of the piece of parchment paper. The paper should extend 4 inches on top and bottom and 2 inches at either side. Slice mushrooms, dice carrot, red pepper and celery. Place vegetables on top of fish. Add the shrimp, heavy cream, lemon juice, salt and pepper. Seal paper around fish. Bake for 30-40 minutes depending on size of fish. Yield: 1-2 servings.

From: **The Garden
at the Lighthouse**
226 East Perry Street
Port Clinton

Sauteed Walleye Pike Wrapped in Napa Cabbage
in a Scallion Butter Sauce

*3 pounds walleye pike fillets,
   cleaned, trimmed and cut into
   6 7-ounce portions*

*salt and pepper
flour
peanut oil
1 head Napa cabbage,
   cleaned and blanched
grated fresh ginger
toasted sesame seeds
1½ cups dry white wine
1 cup water
½ bunch fresh thyme
½ bunch fresh tarragon leaves
3 shallots, minced
1 cup heavy cream
juice of 1 small lemon
¾ pound butter, chilled
   and cut into pieces
1 bunch scallions, minced
   green parts only
1 package Enoki mushrooms,
   trimmed and cut into
   6 portions*

Season walleye portions with generous amount of salt and pepper. Dust lightly with flour. Heat peanut oil until very hot, saute walleye quickly on both sides. Remove from pan and set aside.

Take blanched Napa cabbage and spread out on work surface. Place cooled walleye in the center of the Napa. Sprinkle lightly with the ginger and toasted sesame seeds. Wrap the cabbage around the walleye, completely enclosing the fish.

In a shallow roasting pan, bring ½ cup of the wine, the water and the thyme to a boil. Reduce the heat and let simmer 5 minutes. Place walleye wrapped in cabbage in the pan. Walleye should be just covered with liquid. Place the pan in preheated 400-degree oven and cook for 5-7 minutes.

For the sauce, place 1 cup of the wine, minced shallots and tarragon in a saucepan and reduce until ¼ cup liquid remains. Add the cream and reduce until ½ cup remains. Slowly whisk butter into mixture over low heat. Add lemon juice and salt and pepper to taste. Strain the sauce and add minced scallions.

To serve, nap a heated plate with the sauce. Place the walleye in the center, garnish the top with sauteed Enoki mushrooms. Yield: 6 servings.

From: **Sammy's**
1400 West 10th Street
Cleveland

Vegetables

Vegetables

Vegetables have come a long way from the days of being the food every child left some of, if not all, on the plate. They have also emerged from simply garnishing the more serious food of the entree course. So many attractive, appetizing ways of fixing vegetables have come our way that they are becoming favorites and it's easy to get children to eat them.

Ohio chefs, like the rest of the country, have come up with some refreshing ideas for vegetables. Here they are, everything from eggplant calzone to sweet and white potato dauphinoise. Buon Appetito!

Welshfield Glazed Carrots

The Welshfield Inn was once owned by the village postmaster and was a station on the underground railroad.

1 medium can carrots, sliced
1½ cups pineapple juice
2 tablespoons orange juice
*   concentrate*
2 tablespoons fresh lemon juice
½ cup sugar
¼ cup cornstarch

Drain the carrots and reserve the juice. Combine all of the other ingredients, except the cornstarch, in a saucepan and bring to a boil. Take one cup of the carrot juice and the cornstarch and blend together. Add to the ingredients in the saucepan to thicken the sauce. Add a little diced lemon and orange. Serve hot. Yield: 6 servings.

From: **The Welshfield Inn**
Route 422
Welshfield

Eggplant Calzone

Eggplant Marinade:
1 large eggplant, peeled and
    cubed 1 inch
2 cups olive oil
3 tablespoons honey
1 cup peanut oil
1 bunch fresh basil
1 bunch fresh thyme

Pizza Dough:
6 cups flour
2 tablespoons salt
2 tablespoons honey
¼ cup olive oil
1 ounce fresh yeast
2 cups lukewarm water

Calzones:
eggplant
12 ounces marinara sauce*
12 ounces mozzarella cheese
12 cloves chopped garlic
12 sprigs basil
12 sprigs thyme

*see "The Joy of Cooking" for a
good basic marinara sauce.

For the eggplant, marinate the cubed eggplant in the other ingredients, which have been well blended, overnight. Grill or broil eggplant prior to using in calzones.

To make the pizza dough, mix the flour, salt, honey and olive oil together. Add the yeast, dissolved in the warm water, and mix until the dough is thoroughly blended and pulls away from the side of the bowl. Put in a warm place, cover with a clean towel and let rise. Punch down and let rise again—on second rise it is ready to use. This recipe will make 9 6-inch pizza rounds.

Preheat oven to 400 degrees. Roll out a 6-inch circular pizza dough. Brush with olive oil. Place in the center 4 ounces of the grilled eggplant, 2 ounces of the marinara sauce, and 2 ounces of the mozzarella cheese. Top with 2 cloves of the chopped garlic, which has been roasted in olive oil in the oven at 350 degrees for 20 minutes, 2 sprigs each of the thyme and basil. Fold dough over and pinch the edges. Brush with olive oil and bake in the oven for 8-10 minutes until golden brown. Brush with olive oil, garnish with fresh basil and serve. Yield: 6 servings.

From: **The 10th Street
Cafe & Market**
1400 West 10th Street
Cleveland

Eggplant Fettucini Alfredo

1½ pounds fettucini noodles
2 medium eggplant, peeled
  and cubed
6 tablespoons butter
1 medium onion, diced fine
2 cloves garlic, chopped
1 cup choppped green onions
1 tablespoon salt
1 tablespoon pepper
1¼ teaspoon each parsley,
  oregano, basil, thyme, chervil,
  marjoram
2 cups heavy cream
½ cup sour cream
1 cup freshly grated
  Parmesan cheese

Cook the fettucini noodles in boiling salted water to which you have added 1 teaspoon olive oil to prevent the noodles sticking. Cook until al dente.

Saute the eggplant and the onions in the butter and garlic with the herbs, salt and pepper until the eggplant and onions are soft. Add the heavy cream and bring to a boil. Add the sour cream and bring back to a boil. Add the Parmesan cheese, stirring continuously until the sauce thickens. Add the fettucini noodles, which you have drained, and toss to mix well. Season to taste and serve. Yield: 6 servings.

From: **The Fig Tree**
          909 Vine Street
          Cincinnati

Creamed Spinach

1 pound frozen spinach, chopped
2 tablespoons butter
1 teaspoon salt
½ teaspoon white pepper
2 cups heavy cream
1 tablespoon ground nutmeg

Thaw spinach. Place in food processor and grind until fine. Place spinach in a large towel and squeeze out excess water. Place spinach in a large heavy saucepan. Add the butter, salt and pepper. Heat on medium low heat, stirring occasionally. In a small, heavy bottomed saucepan heat cream and nutmeg until bubbles form around the edges of the cream. When spinach is thoroughly heated, gradually add the cream to the spinach, stirring constantly until all the cream has been incorporated. Place in an oven proof dish and put in 200-degree oven until ready to use.

From: **Chester's Road House**
9678 Montgomery Road
Montgomery

Sweet and White Potatoes Dauphinoise

2 medium russet potatoes
2 medium yams or sweet potatoes
1 clove garlic, crushed
3 tablespoons unsalted butter
1½ cups heavy cream
½ cup bread crumbs

Peel and parboil the potatoes, being careful not to overcook. Drain and slice thinly, using the food processor, if you have one, when they are cool enough to handle.

Preheat the oven to 350 degrees. Butter a 2-quart baking dish, rub with crushed garlic. Layer the sliced potatoes, a layer of white, then a layer of sweet potato. Season with salt and pepper between the layers, top with the breadcrumbs. Pour the heavy cream over and bake until golden brown and potatoes are tender, about 35 minutes. Yield: 8-10 servings.

From: **Lock 24 Restaurant**
State Route 154
Elkton

Glazed Winter Vegetables Julienne

4 medium carrots
2 medium turnips
1 large rutabaga
2 ounces butter
2 ounces honey
¼ teaspoon caraway seeds
salt and pepper to taste

Wash, peel and julienne vegetables. Blanch the vegetables in lightly salted, boiling water until just tender.

Refresh under cold water and then ice, holding for service.

Heat the butter in a large saute pan. Add the vegetables and saute until heated through. Add the honey and salt and pepper to taste. Toss the mixture with the caraway seeds, serve hot.

From: **The Chadwick Inn**
301 River Road
Maumee

Salads & Salad Dressings

Salads and Salad Dressings

The inventiveness of Ohio's chefs is nowhere more available than in the salads and salad dressings. There is something here for everyone, from elaborate to simple.

Curry, pasta, seafood, even duck are ingredients in some of these salads. There's a slaw made from broccoli. Salads for entertaining and for family dining.

Broccoli Slaw

2 medium green peppers
2 small onions
6 cups broccoli stems,
   peeled and grated
1 teaspoon salt
½ teaspoon pepper
1⅓ cups French dressing*

Note—Use Oma's French Dressing featured in this chapter. If you're concerned with calories use a bottled low calorie dressing or a simple vinaigrette.

Chop the green pepper and onion fine; combine with grated broccoli. Stir in salt, pepper and French dressing. Cover the bowl tightly with plastic wrap and chill several hours before serving to blend the flavors. Stir before serving.

Serve broccoli slaw on a lettuce leaf garnished with black olive and a sprig of parsley.

Save the broccoli stems the next time you cook fresh broccoli and make broccoli slaw.

From: **The Inn at Honey Run**
6920 County Road 203
Millersburg

Caesar Salad

Caesar Dressing:

2 ounces anchovies
1½ ounces fresh garlic
3 egg yolks
1 pint virgin olive oil
1 cup red wine vinegar
3 ounces Dijon-style mustard
2 teaspoons salt
1 teaspoon white pepper
1 tablespoon Worcestershire
   sauce

Caesar Salad:

2 large heads romaine
   lettuce, trimmed and cleaned
½ quart caesar dressing
1 cup freshly grated
   Parmesan cheese
2 cups seasoned croutons

Puree anchovies and garlic in blender until they make a fine paste. Set aside. Whip egg yolks in a large mixing bowl until lemon colored, light and fluffy. Add oil and vinegar, beginning and ending with the oil. These should be added in a thin stream. Add remaining ingredients and continue mixing on low speed until all ingredients have been incorporated. Store in a non-reactive container in the refrigerator until ready to use. Yield: 1 quart or 16 2-ounce servings.

Cut romaine into small, bite-size pieces. Place in large bowl. Add the caesar dressing and toss until each piece is lightly coated. Place on 8 chilled salad plates. Sprinkle the Parmesan cheese over the salad and top with the croutons. Yield: 8 servings.

From: **Chester's Road House**
9678 Montgomery Road
Montgomery

Curried Chicken Salad

Salad:
3 pounds chicken breasts,
* boneless, poached*
½ pound raisins, plumped
1 green apple (Granny Smith)
* cut in ½-inch cubes*
1 red apple (firm), cut in
* ½-inch cubes*
1 pear, cut in ½-inch cubes
½ cup unsweetened coconut,
* toasted*
¼ Spanish onion, julienned
½ pound celery, bias cut
½ can pineapple chunks

Dressing:
1½ cups mayonnaise
¼ cup honey
⅛ cup curry powder

Poach the chicken breasts, cool. Remove the skin and dice into ½-inch cubes. Cover the raisins with boiling water and plump. Drain well.

Dice apples and pear. Place in acidulated water. (Water to which lemon juice or vinegar has been added—this prevents the fruit from discoloring.)

Preheat oven to 250 degrees. Place the coconut on a cookie sheet and place in oven. Toast lightly until golden brown.

Combine all the ingredients together.

Mix together the mayonnaise, honey and curry powder and add to the rest of the ingredients. Mix thoroughly and chill. Yield: Approximately 8 servings.

From: **Katzinger's**
          Delicatessen
          475 South Third Street
          Columbus

Warm Duck Sausage Salad
with Black Forest Mushrooms

Duck Sausage:
1 4-pound duckling,
  boned and skinned
¾ pound lean pork
¾ pound veal stew meat
½ pound fat back
2 minced shallots
2 cloves garlic, minced
¾ teaspoon dried rosemary
¼ teaspoon chopped red pepper
1 jigger applejack brandy
¾ cup white wine
salt and freshly ground
  black pepper

Duck Stock:
Reserved duck bones
1 medium carrot
1 medium onion
1 rib celery
1 tomato
¼ cup red wine vinegar
1 clove garlic
1 bay leaf
½ cup port wine

Remove skin from duck, be careful not to puncture skin except for wing and leg openings. Set aside. Put duck meat, pork, veal and fat back through a grinder with medium sized holes. In a rectangular stainless steel pan mix the meat with shallots, garlic, rosemary, red pepper, brandy, salt and pepper, and white wine. Preheat oven to 350 degrees. Cut the reversed duck skin in half. Form the meat mixture into sausage like cylinders. Wrap the duck skin around the sausages and tie securely with kitchen twine. Place sausage in a roasting pan with a little water and roast in oven for an hour and 15 minutes. The sausage should not be cooked dry. Remove from the oven and set aside in a warm place.

Chop duck bones and place in a 450-degree oven until they acquire a nice brown color. Pour off excess fat and add onion, carrot, celery and tomato. Roast for another 20 minutes. Place the solid contents into a stockpot. Pour off any excess fat in the roasting pan and deglaze with red wine vinegar and red port wine. Add this liquid to the solid ingredients in the stockpot. Add cold water until it covers all ingredients. Bring to a boil and simmer for 3½ hours. Strain, pressing all liquid from vegetables and continue cooking until slightly thickened, like syrup.

Mixed Salad:

2 bunches arugula
2 bunches mâche
1 small head curly endive
1 head endive, julienned
2 heads radicchio
½ cup vinaigrette, made with
    extra virgin olive oil and 1
    tablespoon Dijon-style mustard
1 head Bibb lettuce
1 small bunch watercress,
    trimmed of large stems
½ pound Black Forest or
    Shitake mushrooms

Select 12 outer leaves from the radicchio and set aside. Wash the salad greens and pat dry or put in salad spinner. Tear into nice size pieces. Place into salad bowl and toss with the vinaigrette.

Arrange reserved radicchio leaves in a triangular pattern on each plate. Divide the mixed greens into equal portions and place on top of the radicchio base. Slice the duck sausage at a diagonal and attractively arrange 4 to 6 thin slices on top of the salad. Sprinkle mushrooms over and put 3 tablespoons of hot duck stock over the salad. Yield: 4 servings.

From: **Ristorante Giovanni**
25550 Chagrin Boulevard
Cleveland

Pasta Salad

1 cup sun-dried tomatoes
½ pound pasta, cooked al dente
1½ cups sliced fresh mushrooms
1 cup sliced green onions
1 cup chopped fresh tomatoes
2 cups cooked chicken, julienned
2 cups cooked broccoli florettes
8 ounces goat cheese,
  (chevre) crumbled
Parmesan cheese to taste

Drain the dried tomatoes and cut into strips. Toss pasta, vegetables, chicken and chevre with Herb Vinaigrette Dressing. Add Parmesan cheese to taste.

Herb Vinaigrette Dressing:

⅔ cup wine vinegar
2-3 garlic cloves, crushed
2 tablespoons Dijon-style
  mustard
2 teaspooons freshly grated
  black pepper
¼ cup Parmesan cheese
1 cup chopped fresh basil
⅔ cup olive oil
⅔ cup salad oil
1½ teaspoons salt

Combine vinegar, garlic, mustard, pepper, cheese and basil. Set aside for 30 minutes to allow flavors to blend. Add oils to vinegar mixture and blend well. Yield: 2 cups.

From:

**The Heritage
Restaurant**
7664 Wooster Pike
Cincinnati

Salmon Caesar Salad

12 ounces salmon
½ cup water
½ cup chablis
salt to taste
3 tablespoons lemon juice
freshly ground black pepper

1 head romaine lettuce, washed
   and cut into bite-size pieces
1 cup seasoned croutons
1 cup caesar salad dressing
4 tablespoons freshly grated
   Parmesan cheese

Poach the salmon in the water, wine, lemon juice, salt and pepper for 10-12 minutes, just until cooked. Remove from liquid and cool. Reserved liquid may be frozen for later use. When salmon is cooked, flake.

Toss romaine, croutons, salmon and Parmesan cheese with the caesar dressing.

From: **The Watermark
Restaurant**
1250 Old River Road
Cleveland

Shrimp Pasta Salad

1 pound pasta
1½ pounds cooked shrimp
1 cup black olives
4 red peppers
3 green peppers
3 carrots
2 red onions

Dressing:
4 heads garlic
3 bunches fresh dill
8 lemons
2½ cups olive oil

Cook pasta till al dente. Drain, set aside. Cut olives in half the long way. Julienne the vegetables. Cut shrimp in bite-size pieces. Toss vegetables, shrimp and olives with pasta.

Juice lemons, peel and mince garlic. In blender or food processor, blend lemon juice and garlic. Add olive oil cup by cup so the dressing is fully combined. Add dill and blend thoroughly. Season with salt and pepper.

Pour dressing over salad. Chill. Season to taste. Yield: 12-15 servings.

From: **The 10th Street Market & Cafe**
1400 West 10th Street
Cleveland

Shrimp Pasta Salad
with Spicy Garlic Mayonnaise

Spicy Garlic Mayonnaise:
4 medium cloves garlic
½ pimento, seeded
3 egg yolks
1 cup olive oil
1 teaspoon salt
¼ teaspoon pepper

1 pound tri-color rotini
1 pound shrimp, cooked
1 red bell pepper, diced
4 green onions, thinly sliced
¼ cup chopped parsley
2 tablespoons capers, drained
½ cup Spicy Garlic Mayonnaise
2 tablespoons basic vinaigrette

In food processor or blender, puree garlic cloves. Add pimento and egg yolks and blend. Slowly pour in olive oil in a fine, steady stream until sauce is thick and smooth and all the oil has been added. Add the salt and pepper. Taste for seasoning. Refrigerate in a tightly covered container until ready to use.

Cook pasta in a large pot of salted, boiling water for about 10 minutes or until al dente. Drain and remove to a bowl of ice water. Drain thoroughly.

In a small bowl combine the mayonnaise with the vinaigrette and whisk well.

In a large bowl combine the shrimp, pepper, green onions, parsley and capers with the mayonnaise vinaigrette. Serve on leaf lettuce. Yield: 6 servings.

From: **The Watermark Restaurant**
1250 Old River Road
Cleveland

Wild Rice Waldorf Salad

1 cup wild rice, cooked
6 crisp apples, cored and chopped
1 cup walnuts, chopped
4 ribs celery, diced
½ cup pineapple chunks, chopped

Dressing:
6 ounces mayonnaise
6 ounces sour cream
2 tablespoons pineapple juice
1 cup mayonnaise
⅔ cup sugar
¼ cup cider vinegar

Cook wild rice and cool.

Chop apples and put in acidulated water (water that contains either lemon juice or vinegar to retard discoloration of fruit). Drain well. Add the walnuts, celery and pineapple to the apples.

Combine all the ingredients for the dressing and mix well. Combine the dressing with the salad ingredients, add the wild rice and mix well.

Check for dryness, add more dressing if necessary.

From: **Katzinger's Delicatessen**
475 South Third Street
Columbus

House Dijon Vinaigrette

½ cup wine vinegar
½ teaspoon salt
¼ teaspoon white pepper
½ tablespoon Dijon-style mustard
½ teaspoon dried tarragon leaves
pinch garlic powder
1 cup salad oil

Combine all ingredients except salad oil. Mix well. Slowly add the salad oil and mix or shake to combine. Mixture will separate when stored. Shake before using.

From: **Hulbert's Restaurant**
1033 Bridge Street
Ashtabula

Oma's French Dressing

1 cup mayonnaise
²/₃ cup sugar
¼ cup cider vinegar
2 tablespoons vegetable oil
1 tablespoon mustard
¼ cup ketchup
⅛ teaspoon garlic powder
2 teaspoons lemon juice
¼ teaspoon salt
¼ teaspoon paprika
¼ pepper
⅛ teaspoon hot pepper sauce

In covered blender at medium speed, blend all ingredients until thoroughly mixed. Store in tightly covered jar in refrigerator. Stir or shake well before using.

For fruit salads, substitute grapefruit or lemon juice for the vinegar.

For the best results with salad, place the dressing in the bottom of the bowl with the greens layered on top. Toss at the table, just before serving. Pass the pepper grinder.

From: **The Inn at Honey Run**
6920 County Road 203
Millersburg

Desserts

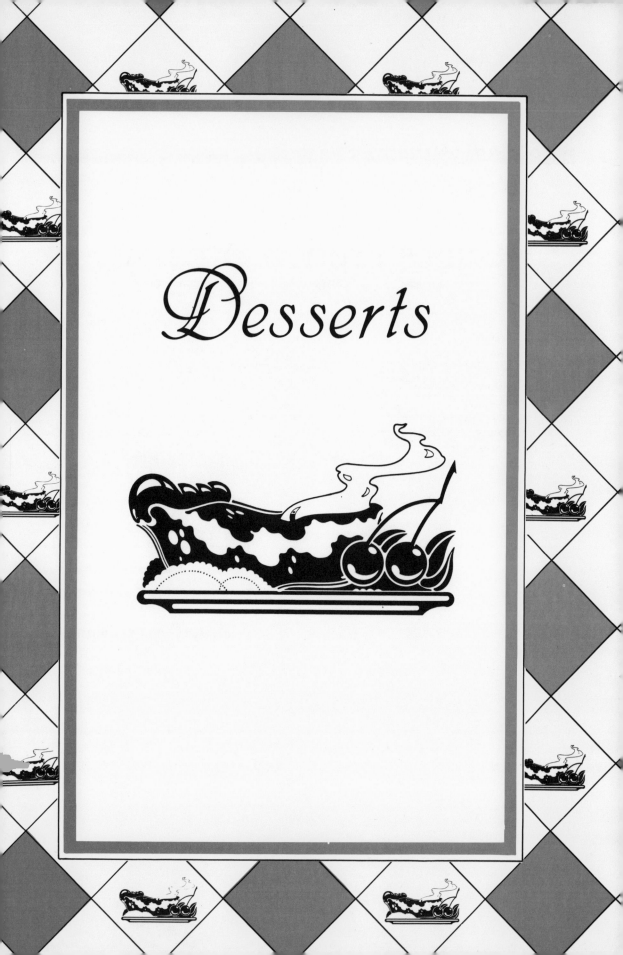

Desserts

What need be said about dessert? That it is supposed to be the satisfactory conclusion to the meal.
It should be something of a reward, not for eating
all your vegetables, but just for living.

The best desserts have something of the slightly
forbidden about them, an indulgence we would not
normally allow ourselves. That is what makes
them special and what makes us almost invariably
order dessert when we go out for a meal. That, and
the knowledge that good restaurants "do" desserts
especially well.

That being so, here are some of Ohio's best desserts. There's plenty of eggs, cream, butter and
sugar, as well as dark chocolate, various liqueurs
and other slightly iniquitous delicacies. Enjoy!

Hot Apple Cake

½ cup butter
1 cup sugar
3 eggs, beaten
1½ cups flour
1½ teaspoons baking powder
⅛ teaspoon salt
1 teaspoon vanilla
8 medium tart apples

Topping:
¼ cup butter
½ cup sugar
½ cup flour
cinnamon to taste

Preheat the oven to 350 degrees. Cream the butter and sugar together until light and fluffy. Add the beaten eggs and beat until light. Sift the dry ingredients, combine the mixtures and add the vanilla.

Pour the dough into a well greased 8 x 11 inch pan. Pare and cut tart apples in ⅛'s. Stick the fruit halfway into the dough in rows, using plenty of fruit. Sprinkle liberally with cinnamon.

Cream the butter with the sugar, cut in the flour with a pastry fork until the mixture is crumbly. Sprinkle over the top and bake in the oven for 45 minutes. Yield: 6-8 servings.

From: **The Apple Farm
Restaurant**
262 Pearl Road
Brunswick

Apple in the Pajama

1 tablespoon sugar
1 teaspoon raisins
⅛ teaspoon cinnamon
1 tablespoon orange or apricot
   marmalade
1 medium apple (Jonathan or
   Winesap), peeled and cored
1 6x6 inch piece puff pastry
1 egg
½ cup milk

Preheat oven to 350 degrees. Mix sugar, raisins, cinnamon and marmalade together and place in the cored apple. Wrap the apple in puff pastry and press the edges together to seal.

Mix the egg and milk together to make egg wash. Brush puff pastry with egg wash.

Bake in 350 degree oven for 30-45 minutes. Sprinkle with powdered sugar and serve garnished with whipped cream.

From: **The Golden Lamb**
227 South Broadway
Lebanon

Apple Pie
with Shaker Crumb Topping

1 9-inch pie shell
3 cups apples, peeled, cored
  and sliced
1 cup sugar
¼ teaspoon nutmeg
¼ teaspoon cinnamon
⅓ cup flour

Topping:
½ cup butter
½ cup brown sugar
1 cup flour

Preheat oven to 350 degrees. Place the apples in the pie shell. Sprinkle with the sugar, flour, cinnamon and nutmeg.

Melt the butter in a saucepan and mix in flour and brown sugar to make a crumbly mixture.

Top pie with this mixture and bake in the oven for approximately 30 minutes.

From: **The Golden Lamb**
          227 South Broadway
          Lebanon

Beggar's Pudding with Orange Vanilla Sauce

12 ounces white bread torn
  into pieces
6 eggs
5 ounces sugar
1/4 teaspoon salt
1 teaspoon cinnamon
1 teaspoon nutmeg
1 tablespoon vanilla
3 1/2 cups scalded milk
1/2 cup raisins
1/2 cup pecans

Orange Vanilla Sauce:
8 ounces heavy cream
1/2 cup sugar
1/2 teaspoon vanilla
1/4 teaspoon salt
3 egg yolks
1 ounce Grand Marnier

Preheat oven to 350 degrees. For the pudding, arrange 1/2 of the bread in a well greased cake pan. Sprinkle 1/2 of the raisins and pecans over the bread.

Mix together the eggs, sugar, salt and vanilla, gradually stir in the hot milk, whisking briskly to keep the eggs from cooking. Pour 1/2 of the custard mixture over the bread, then add the rest of the bread and the rest of the custard. Sprinkle the remaining raisins and pecans on top and sprinkle with a little cinnamon and nutmeg.

Put the cake pan in a larger pan, which is partially filled with hot water, and put in the oven. Bake for 35-40 minutes. Serve warm.

For the sauce, heat the cream, sugar, vanilla and salt together. Whisk in the egg yolks one at a time. Cook over low heat just until the sauce starts to thicken. Do NOT boil. Remove from stove and add the Grand Marnier. Serve over the Beggar's Pudding.

From: **The Chadwick Inn**
                301 River Road
                Maumee

Classic Genoise

6 eggs
1 cup sugar
pinch of salt
1 cup flour, sifted
½ cup butter, melted
    and cooled
½ teaspoon vanilla

Butter and flour two 8- or 9-inch cake pans. Preheat oven to 375 degrees.

Place the eggs, still in shell, in a bowl of hot tap water while assembling the remaining ingredients. Warming the eggs in the bowl will make it easier to achieve maximum volume in the finished product.

Place the flour and salt in a small bowl. Similarly, combine the butter and vanilla in their own container.

Rinse a large mixing bowl with hot water to warm it. Dry. Crack the eggs into the warmed bowl, add the sugar and beat on high speed until mixture is light, fluffy and very pale (about 5-8 minutes). Using a rubber spatula, carefully fold flour in, not just a few strokes, although flour will not be completely incorporated at this time. Then take the butter and vanilla mixture and completely incorporate all ingredients. It is important to avoid overmixing as this will result in a flat cake. Pour batter into prepared pans. Bake in the oven until the top is browned and the cake begins to pull away from the sides of the pan, about 25-30 minutes. Cool completely before turning out of pans.

For a chocolate genoise, replace ½ cup of the flour with ½ cup of unsweetened, powdered cocoa.

Yield: 2 cakes.

From: **The Bryn Mawr Restaurant**
3758 Lancaster Road
Granville

Chester's Chocolate Miracle Cure

Chester does not say what this is a cure for, but it sounds wonderful enough to cure just about anything!

1 pound German sweet
  chocolate
16 ounces sugar
¼ cup freshly brewed coffee
10 ounces unsalted butter
8 eggs
1 ounces dark rum

Raspberry Sauce:
2 pounds frozen raspberries
2 cups sugar
1 cup water
4 ounces cornstarch
½ pint heavy cream
¼ cup confectioner's sugar
1 teaspoon vanilla extract

For the chocolate cake, first remove the eggs from the refrigerator and allow to come to room temperature. Preheat oven to 350 degrees. Place the chocolate, sugar and coffee in a large saucepan. Heat over medium low heat until chocolate has melted and sugar has dissolved. Place chocolate mixture in a large mixing bowl and mix on medium high speed. Add the butter, a small piece at a time, to the chocolate mixture. Continue mixing until all of the butter has been incorporated. On medium high speed, add 1 egg at a time to the chocolate butter mixture until well incorporated. Add the rum and mix until thoroughly combined. Grease a spring form pan, line with parchment paper. Pour batter into pan and bake in oven for 1½ hours or until toothpick inserted in center of cake comes out clean.

Cool the cake until it reaches room temperature and then remove from pan. Serve with raspberry sauce and whipped cream.

For the raspberry sauce, place the thawed raspberries and sugar in a large saucepan. Heat on medium heat until it comes to a boil. Stir occasionally. Pour through a strainer, reserving the juice. Throw away the seeds, return the sauce to the heat.

In a small bowl combine the water and cornstarch until it makes a thin, fine paste.

Using a wire whisk, slowly pour the cornstarch and water mixture into the raspberry sauce. Continue whisking until all the cornstarch has been absorbed.

Cook for 15-20 minutes or until the starchy taste has disappeared. Place in a non-reactive container until it has cooled to room temperature. Keep refrigerated until ready for service.

Whip the cream until soft peaks form. Add the sugar and vanilla and continue whipping on high speed until stiff peaks form.

To serve, cut the cake, dipping the knife in hot water each time. Place 3 ounces of the raspberry sauce on the bottom of each chilled dessert plate. Put a slice of the cake on the sauce with a large dollop of the whipped cream topped with a fresh strawberry. Yield: 8 servings.

From: **Chester's Road House**
9678 Montgomery Road
Montgomery

Chocolate Terrine

4 ounces semi-sweet chocolate
11 ounces bittersweet chocolate
1 cup strong coffee
7 eggs, separated
12 ounces butter, softened
1/3 cup cognac
1 orange, zest only

In the top of a double boiler, melt the 2 chocolates with the coffee. Whisk together until completely melted and blended.

Add 3 of the egg yolks, blend well. Slowly incorporate the butter, blending well. Add the rest of the egg yolks along with the cognac and orange zest. Blend well. Remove from the heat and let stand for 5 minutes, stirring occasionally.

Whip the egg whites to stiff peaks. Carefully fold the egg whites into the chocolate mixture, using a rubber spatula. Do not overmix. Once the 2 mixtures are incorporated, pour into a mold and let stand in the refrigerator for at least 24 hours.

To unmold the chocolate terrine, place the mold in a warm water bath for about 30 seconds. Remove the mold from the water and invert onto a sheet pan lined with parchment paper. Slice and serve, garnished with candied orange peel or fresh raspberries.

From: **Ziggy's**
Continental Restaurant
3140 Riverside Drive
Columbus

The Flourless Chocolate Cake

10 ounces semi-sweet chocolate
4 ounces unsalted butter
6 eggs, separated
1 cup sugar
2 teaspoons creme de cacao
½ teaspoon vanilla
1 pinch cream of tartar
pinch of salt
butter
flour

Vanilla Sauce:
2½ cups milk
½ vanilla bean
6 egg yolks
½ cup sugar
½ lemon peel

Preheat oven to 375 degrees. Butter and flour a 8½-inch springform pan. Melt the chocolate with the butter in a double boiler. Keep melted chcolate warm. Beat the egg yolks in a mixing bowl at high speed, gradually adding ¾ cup sugar. Beat until the yolk mixture is pale yellow in color, about 4 minutes. Add melted chocolate mixture to yolk mixture and beat until completely smooth. Then add the creme de cacao, adding in the vanilla at the same time. Beat the egg whites with a pinch of salt and a pinch of cream of tartar until soft peaks form. Gradually add remaining ¼ cup of sugar into the whites. Continue beating until stiff, but not dry. Fold whites into the chocolate mixture and pour batter evenly into the springform pan.

Bake for 15 minutes at 375 degrees, then reduce the oven temperature to 350 degrees. Bake another 15 minutes. Reduce the oven temperature to 250 degrees and bake 30 minutes longer. Turn off the oven, prop open the door, and allow the cake to remain in the oven for 30 minutes. Remove the cake from oven and cover with lightly dampened towel. Let stand 10 minutes. Remove the towel and cool cake completely. Press top of cake lightly to smooth the top. Remove the springform pan, inverting the cake onto a serving platter. Serve with Vanilla Sauce.

For the sauce, combine the vanilla bean and milk. Combine the egg yolks and sugar with a balloon whisk, slowly adding the vanilla flavored milk and grated lemon peel. Heat the mixture until it coats the back of a spoon lightly. Put a serving of sauce on each plate and place a piece of the cake on the sauce. Yield: 8-10 servings.

From: **Ristorante Giovanni**
25550 Chagrin Boulevard
Cleveland

Fruited Mousse

2 cups heavy cream
2 cups fruit, fresh or frozen
¼ cup sugar or to taste*

*The amount of sugar will depend on the fruit used, whether it is fresh or frozen and on individual taste.

Place fruit and sugar in a heavy saucepan. Cook the fruit down to a thick preserve-like consistency, adjusting the sweetness to taste. Remove from the heat and cool to room temperature, stirring occasionally.

Meanwhile, whip the cream until very stiff but avoid overwhipping as this results in butter, which you don't want. Reserve about ½ cup of this for garnish.

When fruit is completely cool, fold carefully into the whipped cream. Spoon into wine or sherbet glasses and garnish with a dollop of plain whipped cream and a bit of fresh fruit.

High acid fruits such as citrus and pineapple should be avoided. The berry family is best for this elegant but simple dessert. Yield: 6 servings.

From: **The Bryn Mawr Restaurant**
3758 Lancaster Road
Granville

Old-fashioned Bread Pudding

2 cups milk, scalded
4 cups coarse bread crumbs
¼ cup butter, melted
½ cup sugar
4 eggs, slightly beaten
¼ teaspoon salt
½ cup raisins
1 teaspoon cinnamon or nutmeg

Preheat the oven to 350 degrees. Cool the scalded milk, add in the melted butter, sugar, and the eggs, salt, raisins and cinnamon.

Put the bread in a buttered 1½-quart casserole. Pour the milk mixture over the bread and bake in the oven for 40-45 minutes or until a silver knife inserted in the middle comes out clean. Serve warm with hard sauce or cream. Yield: 6 servings.

From: **The Welshfield Inn**
Route 422
Welshfield

Pâté à Chou
with Crème Parisienne

Cream Puff Dough:
1 cup water
½ cup butter
½ teaspoon salt
1 teaspoon sugar
1 cup flour
½ teaspoon baking powder
4 eggs

Creme Parisienne:
1½ cups heavy cream
2 ounces semi-sweet chocolate,
chopped

Preheat oven to 400 degrees. It is important to have the oven hot.

For the cream puffs, combine the water, butter, salt and sugar in a heavy saucepan. Have the flour and baking powder sifted and ready near the stove. Bring mixture in saucepan to a boil; add the flour all at once, remove from heat and blend until the dough becomes a smooth, homogenous mass. Continue to work the dough until little or no steam rises from it.

Transfer the dough to the bowl of an electric mixer. With the whip attachment, beat dough on high speed. Add the eggs, one at a time, mixing thoroughly and scraping down the sides of the bowl after each addition. Finally, beat for 2-3 minutes longer until a smooth, shiny consistency is achieved.

Prepare a cookie sheet by lining with parchment paper or coating lightly with spray-on cooking oil. using a large spoon, drop the pate a chou (cream puff) dough into mounds approximately 2 inches apart, smoothing any peaks or edges with a spoon. Bake at 400 degrees until the puffs rise fully and are nicely browned. Reduce the heat to 350 degrees, prop the oven door open about 1 inch and bake an additional 5-10 minutes.

When broken open the cream puff should be dry and hollow. If inside is moist and stretchy, dry in the oven an additional 5 minutes. Cool the puffs, slice them in half, fill with Creme Parisienne, replace tops. Sprinkle with powdered sugar and serve.

DESSERTS

For the Creme Parisienne, place the pieces of chocolate and the cream in a bowl over boiling water. Heat, stirring occasionally, until chocolate is melted and dispersed through the cream. Remove the bowl from heat and place in a larger bowl filled with ice. Using a wire whisk or electric hand mixer, whip the cream until it is stiff and holds a good peak. Use it to fill the cream puffs. Yield: 15-20 cream puffs. Uncut, these puffs will last for a week or so stored in an airtight container.

From: **The Bryn Mawr
Restaurant**
3758 Lancaster Road
Granville

Peanut Butter Cream Pie

1 large package vanilla
    pudding and pie mix
2 cups milk
½ cup crunchy peanut butter
½ pint heavy cream
1 9-inch pie shell, baked
1 banana, sliced
1 tablespoon ground walnuts
chocolate syrup or sauce
whipped cream

Follow the directions on the package of the pie mix, cooking with the milk and peanut butter. Cool. Whip the cream till stiff peaks form and fold gently into the pudding mix. Fill the pie shell and freeze.

About an hour before serving, remove the pie from the freezer. When ready to serve, slice banana on top of each pie slice, top with additional whipped cream, add the chocolate syrup or sauce and the ground walnuts.

From: **Dobie's Corner**
Ghent Square
843 North Cleveland-Massillion Road
Ghent

Pumpkin Mousse

1 pint heavy cream
4 egg yolks
5 ounces superfine sugar
½ teaspoon cinnamon
½ teaspoon pumpkin pie spice*
1 cup pumpkin

*pumpkin spice is a blend of cinnamon, nutmeg, allspice and ginger.

Whip the cream until it forms stiff peaks. Be careful not to overbeat or you'll end up with butter. Set the whipped cream aside.

Combine the egg yolks, sugar, cinnamon, pumpkin pie spice, and pumpkin. Blend all ingredients thoroughly. Gently fold the whipped cream into the pumpkin mixture, using a rubber spatula. Serve topped with more whipped cream. Yield: 12 6-ounce servings.

From: **The Garden at the Lighthouse**
226 East Perrry Street
Port Clinton

Raspberry Cloud Mousse

2 envelopes unflavored gelatin
¼ cup water
2 packages frozen raspberries,
  thawed
1½ teaspoons lemon juice
¼ cup sugar
4 egg whites
dash salt
¼ cup sugar
1 cup heavy cream

Soften the gelatin in the cold water. Combine the raspberries, softened gelatin, the first amount of sugar, and lemon juice in a saucepan. Cook, stirring constantly over low heat until the gelatin dissolves. Remove from heat and cool until slightly thickened. Beat the egg whites and salt until soft peaks form. Gradually add the second amount of sugar and beat just until stiff peaks form. Whip cream to stiff peaks. Fold beaten egg whites gently into the whipped cream. Fold raspberries into mixture, leaving a few white streaks for a cloud effect. Spoon into sherbet dishes. Top with additional whipped cream if desired and garnish with fresh mint leaves. Yield: 10 servings.

From: **The Inn at Honey Run**
6920 County Road 203
Millersburg

Tirami Su

This literally means "Lift me up" or "Pick me up" in Italian. The dish has been served in Italy for at least two centuries and is the pride of every Italian grandmother. Try it and you'll see why!

3 egg yolks
7 tablespoons sugar
1¼ pounds mascarpone cheese*
2 teaspoons amaretto
1 teaspoon vanilla
30 Italian ladyfingers
  (savoiardi)*
1½ cups cooled espresso
½ cup chopped bittersweet
  chocolate
½ cup chopped toasted almonds
1½ pints raspberries
6 mint leaves on stem

*Mascarpone and savoiardi should both be available in Italian groceries or specialty food shops.

Whisk the eggs yolks and sugar in a mixing bowl until the egg yolks turn a pale yellow. Beat in the mascarpone, amaretto and vanilla until the mixture is well mixed and creamy.

Dip 10 of the lady fingers lightly in the cooled espresso and arrange in 2 rows in a flat-bottomed, deep-sided 8 x 12 inch rectangular serving dish. Spread a ⅓ of the mascarpone mixture on top of the layered ladyfingers and sprinkle with a ⅓ of the chopped chocolate and almonds and raspberries. Repeat this layering process 2 more times. Refrigerate until ready to serve. Garnish with remaining raspberries and mint leaves. Yield: 8 servings.

From: **Ristorante Giovanni**
25550 Chagrin Boulevard
Cleveland

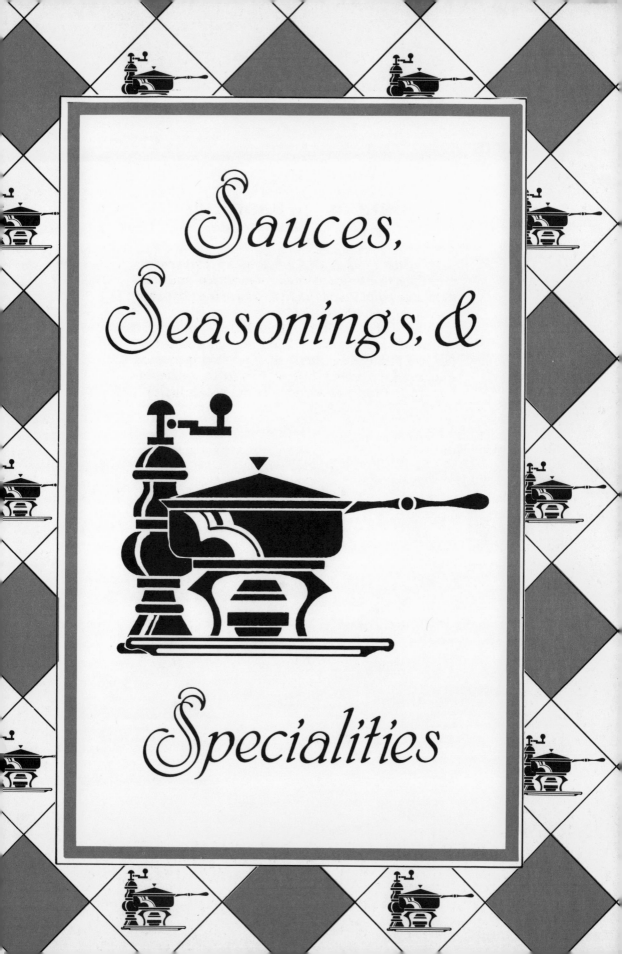

Sauces, Seasonings, & Specialities

Sauces, Seasonings
and Specialties

There are recipes for sauces, for special seasonings used in ethnic cuisines, for example, and other delicacies that just don't fit in any of the neat categories into which we divide our cookbooks.

So here they are, last but definitely not least. If you've always wanted to know how chocolate truffles are made, here they are. If you want to know how to make crème fraîche, here it is, as well as some other tasty evocations of the cook's world.

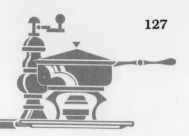

Jerry Hart's
Chocolate Truffles

Good quality chocolate is the secret to successful truffles.

*1 pound good quality
   bittersweet chocolate*
1 cup heavy cream

Chop the chocolate into ½-inch pieces. Put chopped chocolate into a food processor. Bring heavy cream to a boil in a heavy saucepan. Add the hot cream to the chocolate and process until the chocolate cream mixture is perfectly smooth.

Flavor with the desired liqueur and form into 1-inch balls.

Variations:

One ounce Amaretto, roll in chopped, toasted almonds

One ounce Grand Marnier, 1 teaspoon grated orange rind, roll in unsweetened cocoa powder

One ounce Kahlua and roll in mixture of unsweetened cocoa powder and small amount of instant coffee

One ounce Frangelico and roll in chopped, toasted hazelnuts.

Yield: 40-50 truffles. Spectacular gift!

From: **The Heritage Restaurant**
7664 Wooster Pike
Cincinnati

Crème Fraîche

¾ cup sour cream
1¼ cups heavy cream

Whip the 2 creams together until thoroughly blended. Let sit at room temperature for 2 hours.

Store in a glass jar in the refrigerator. It will keep for at least 1 month. Use it in any recipe that calls for sour cream or whipping cream. It does not curdle when boiled and will give your dishes a distinct taste.

From: **Lock 24 Restaurant**
Route 154
Elkton

Fennel, Red Onion, Jicama and Celery Compote

This makes a wonderful garnish or sauce for grilled or baked fish.

1 small-medium bulb
  fennel, diced
1 small red onion, diced
1 bulb jicama, peeled and diced
2 tablespoons olive oil
¾ cup balsamic vinegar
1 tablespoon garlic
salt and pepper to taste

Combine all ingredients except the balsamic vinegar in a non-reactive saucepan. Cook over low heat for 45-60 minutes or until the vegetables are soft but not overcooked. Add the balsamic vinegar and seasoning, cook for another 10 minutes.

Use this vegetable compote as garnish by making a cordon around a piece of grilled fish, or use as a sauce or relish over the fish.

From: **Rigsby's
Cuisine Volatile**
692 North High Street
Columbus

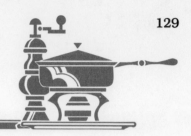

Grapefruit Sorbet

20 (approx.) sugar cubes,
  ½-inch square, (1¾ ounces)
3-4 large grapefruit at
  room temperature
juice of ½ lemon
½ teaspoon white Karo syrup
¼ cup granulated sugar

Rub each side of each sugar cube on the skin of a grapefruit to extract some of the oils, just hard enough to color the cube. Do not rub too hard or the flavor will be bitter.

Halve the grapefruit and squeeze enough juice to get 2 cups plus 2 tablespoons when measured after straining. Grapefruits will yield more juice at room temperature than when chilled.

Combine the sugar cubes with grapefruit and lemon juices. Stir well and set aside until dissolved. Pour mixture into ice cream machine and turn the machine on. Add Karo syrup. Freeze according to manufacturer's instructions. Or, still-freeze: Pour mixture into a shallow metal baking pan and freeze until slushy. Beat with an electric mixer and freeze until firm. Let thaw slightly before serving. For a fluffier texture, beat again. Yield: 4-6 servings.

From: **The 10th Street
Market & Cafe**
1400 West Tenth Street
Cleveland

Toffee Almond Sauce

This makes a perfect gift from your kitchen.

1½ cups light brown sugar
2 cups light corn syrup
½ cup butter
¼ teaspoon salt
2 cups heavy cream
2 tablespoons vanilla
4 cups toasted, sliced almonds

To toast the almonds, spread out on a cookie sheet and toast in the oven at 375 degrees, watching carefully so they brown without burning.

In a large heavy saucepan, combine brown sugar, corn syrup, butter and salt. Bring to a boil. Boil 3 minutes. Add the cream and stir until well blended. Add the vanilla and then the toasted almonds. May be served either at room temperature or warmed. Yield: 6 cups.

From: **The Heritage Restaurant**
7664 Wooster Pike
Cincinnati

Inns & Restaurants

The numbers in parentheses after the name of the restaurant refer to the pages on which recipes from each establishment appear.

Dobie's Corner
Ghent Square
843 North Cleveland-Massillion Road
Ghent (Akron)
216/666-1676
No reservations
Credit cards: V, MC, AE
(4, 28, 121)

Hulbert's Restaurant
1033 Bridge Street
Ashtabula
216/964-2594
No reservations
No credit cards
(10, 17, 103)

The Apple Farm Restaurant
262 Pearl Road
Brunswick
216/225-5576
No reservations
Credit cards: V, MC, AE, DC
(3, 61, 107)

CINCINNATI AREA

Arnold's Bar & Grill
210 East Eighth Street
Cincinnati
513/421-6234
Reservations suggested for six or more
No credit cards
(18, 34, 44)

The Fig Tree
909 Vine Street
Cincinnati
513/241-2344
Reservations suggested
Credit cards: V, MC, AE
(7, 55, 74, 87)

Grammer's Restaurant
1440 Walnut Street
Cincinnati
216/721-6570
Reservations suggested
Credit cards: V, MC, AE
(25, 29)

The Heritage Restaurant
7664 Wooster Pike
Cincinnati
513/561-9300
Reservations suggested
Credit cards: V, MC, AE
(50, 98, 127, 130)

La Maisonette
114 East Sixth Street
Cincinnati
513/721-2260
Advance reservations required
Credit cards: V, MC, AE
(53, 65, 71)

Peerless Mill Inn
319 South Second Street
Miamisburg
513/866-5968
No reservations
Credit cards: V, MC, AE
(6, 35, 57)

CLEVELAND AREA

The Baricelli Inn
2203 Cornell Road
Cleveland
216/791-6500
Reservations necessary
Credit cards: V, MC, AE
(8, 9, 10, 58)

Minh Anh Restaurant
5428 Detroit Avenue
Cleveland
216/961-9671
Reservations preferred
Credit cards: V, MC
(48)

Ristorante Giovanni
25550 Chagrin Boulevard
Cleveland
216/831-8626
Reservations suggested
Credit cards: V, MC,AE
(68, 75, 96, 115, 124)

Sammy's
1400 West 10th Street
Cleveland
216/523-5560
Reservations suggested
Credit cards: V, MC, AE, DC, CB
(42, 82)

The 10th Street Market & Cafe
400 West 10th Street
Cleveland
216/523-1094
Reservations unnecessary
Credit cards: V, MC, AE, DC, CB
(5, 18, 26, 86, 100, 129)

The Watermark
1250 Old River Road
Cleveland
216/241-1600
Reservations advised
Credit cards: V, MC, AE
(52, 99, 101)

COLUMBUS AREA

L'Armagnac Restaurant Francais
121 South Sixth Street
Columbus
614/221-4046
Reservations suggested
Credit cards: V, MC
(27, 36, 77)

Katzinger's Delicatessen
475 South Third Street
(German Village)
Columbus
614/228-DELI
No reservations
No credit cards
(95, 102)

Rigsby's Cuisine Volatile
692 North High Street
Columbus
614/461-7888
Reservations recommended
Credit cards: V, MC, AE
(20, 38, 128)

Ziggy's Continental Restaurant
3140 Riverside Drive
Columbus
614/488-0605
Reservations suggested
Credit cards: V, MC, AE
(15, 29, 36, 114)

L'Auberge
4120 Far Hill Avenue
Dayton
513/299-5536
Reservations suggested
Credit cards: V, MC, AE
(24, 64, 80)

Lock 24 Restaurant
State Route 154
Elkton
216/424-3710
No reservations
Credit cards: V, MC
(12, 33, 54, 78, 89, 128)

The Bryn Mawr Restaurant
3758 Lancaster Road
Granville
614/587-4000
Reservations required
Credit cards: V, MC, AE
(49, 62, 111, 117, 119)

The Golden Lamb
227 South Broadway
Lebanon
513/932-5065
Reservations advised
Credit cards: V, MC, AE, CB, DC
(38, 60, 108, 109)

The Betsey Mills Club Dining Room
300 4th Street
Marietta
614/373-3804
No reservations
Credit cards: V, MC
(6)

The Gun Room at
The Lafayette Hotel
101 Front Street
Marietta
614/373-5522
Reservations suggested
Credit cards: V, MC, AE, DC, CB
(47, 66, 79)

The Inn at Honey Run
6920 County Road 203
Millersburg
216/674-0011
Reservations necessary
No credit cards
(39, 93, 104, 123)

Chester's Road House
9678 Montgomery Road
Montgomery
513/793-8700
Reservations suggested
Credit cards: V, MC, AE
(51, 72, 88, 94, 112)

The Garden at the Lighthouse
226 East Perry Street
Port Clinton
419/732-2151
Reservations recommended in summer
Credit cards: V, MC, AE, DC, CB
(78, 81, 122)

Linardo's Villa
2230 East Main Street
Springfield
513/323-3011
Reservations unnecessary
Credit cards: V, MC, AE, DC, CB
(11)

TOLEDO AREA

The Chadwick Inn
301 River Road
Maumee
419/893-2388
No reservations
Credit cards: V, MC
(19, 43, 90, 110)

Ricardo's
Owens-Illinois Building
One Seagate, Park Level 118
Toledo
419/255-1116
Reservations suggested
Credit cards: V, MC
(56, 63)

The Welshfield Inn
Route 422
Welshfield
216/834-4164
Reservations suggested
Credit cards: V, MC, AE
(23, 85, 118)

Index